To Diane —
I trust your feet got dusty as you walked along with Mary.
Be blessed!
Delores Winegan

MARY,
THE
LORD'S SERVANT

MARY,
THE
LORD'S SERVANT

A novel from the Protestant viewpoint using
Biblical truths, historical facts, and archeological discoveries

DELORES WINEGAR

XULON PRESS

Xulon Press
2301 Lucien Way #415
Maitland, FL 32751
407.339.4217
www.xulonpress.com

© 2019 by Delores Winegar

All rights reserved solely by the author. The author guarantees all contents are original and do not infringe upon the legal rights of any other person or work. No part of this book may be reproduced in any form without the permission of the author. The views expressed in this book are not necessarily those of the publisher.

Unless otherwise indicated, Scripture quotations are taken from the *Holy Bible*, New Living Translation (NLT). Copyright © 1996, 2004, 2015 by Tyndale House Foundation. Used by permission of Tyndale House Publishers, Inc., Carol Stream, Illinois 60188. All rights reserved.

Printed in the United States of America.

ISBN-13: 978-1-5456-7929-6

TABLE OF CONTENTS

Introduction..ix
Map of First Century Israel........................x
List of Characters.....................................xi

CHAPTER ONE: **"Favored"**............................1

CHAPTER TWO: **Travel Days**........................15

CHAPTER THREE: **With Elizabeth**.................31

CHAPTER FOUR: **Mary's Homecoming**...........43

CHAPTER FIVE: **The Parade**........................57

CHAPTER SIX: **Traveling to Bethlehem**........69

CHAPTER SEVEN: **"Would You Like to Hold the Baby?"**..77

CHAPTER EIGHT: **Puzzling Words in Jerusalem**........87

CHAPTER NINE: **Royal Visitors**..................97

CHAPTER TEN: **A New City**......................107

EPILOGUE – 58 years later: **"Every Knee Will Bow"**....115
Appendix..125

INTRODUCTION

Just over 2,000 years ago, Israel was not a free country. It was occupied by the Romans, who ruled the known world in the first century. Their laws were to be obeyed, and many crucifixions were carried out to control lawbreakers.

In this country the Jewish nation called out to the God of their ancestors, Abraham, Isaac, and Jacob. God had given them this land in days of old and had, through the prophets, promised to send a Redeemer, their Messiah. They lived their lives praying for the Messiah to come, envisioning that he would set their country free once again from foreign rule.

Mary was a fourteen-year-old Jewish girl who was dedicated to serving God, now excited to be engaged to marry the new Nazareth resident, Joseph. Mary was joyful, knowing the God she worshipped had granted her desire to marry a God-fearing Israelite also from the tribe of Judah. But her life was radically changed when she was told she would be the mother of the promised Messiah and as she lived with that reality through Jesus' birth, life, and heart-wrenching death.

To assist you, the reader, a map of First Century Israel and a List of Characters follow this Introduction. The author has used some first century terms, such as the money used then, but also some current terms, such as miles and names of months, for easy reading and clarity.

Join Mary on a journey of self-discovery, divine revelation, and the joys and adventures of an anything-but-ordinary life as she becomes the woman God used to alter the course of history as His faithful servant.

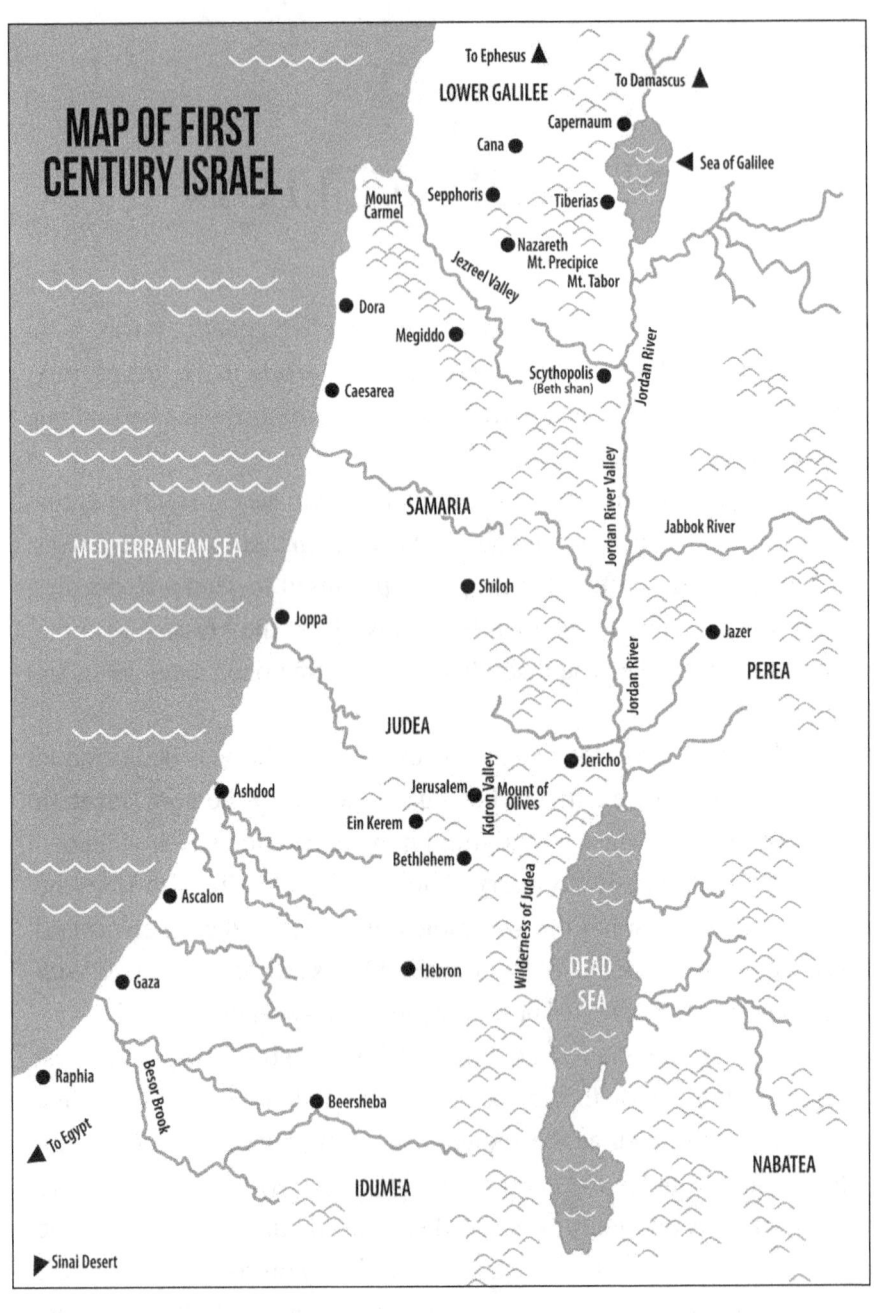

List of Characters

Aaron	Zechariah's friend, also a Levitical priest
Abigail	Widow of Matthat, mother of Heli, grandmother of Mary, called "Buppy"
Amos	Son of Heli and Johanna, brother of Caleb, Salome, Mary, Simon
Anna	Prophetess at the Temple in Jerusalem
Asa	Son of Nathan and Rachel, brother of Elisheba
Azor	Son of Innkeepers, Micah and Ethlan, in Bethlehem
Caleb	Son of Heli and Johanna, brother of Salome, Mary, Amos, Simon
Carmen	Servant of Elizabeth and Zechariah
Eliakim	Jewish leader in Alexandria, Egypt
Elisheba	Infant daughter of Nathan and Rachel, sister of Asa
Elizabeth	Johanna's cousin, wife of Zechariah, mother of John (the Baptist)
Esther	Wife of Nahum, mother of Matthias, Joel, Jessie, Mary's aunt
Ethlan	Wife of Innkeeper Micah, mother of Azor
Hannah	Mary's best friend in Nazareth

Mary, the Lord's Servant

Heli	Husband of Johanna, father of Caleb, Salome, Mary, Amos, Simon
Hirah	Palm date merchant in Jerusalem, husband of Miriam, father of Keren
Jessie	Son of Nahum and Esther, brother of Matthias, Joel
Jesus	Son of God, son of Mary, step-son of Joseph, half-brother of James, Joseph, Judas, Simon, and three sisters
Joel	Son of Nahum and Esther, brother of Matthias, Jessie
Johanna	Wife of Heli, mother of Caleb, Salome, Mary, Amos, Simon
John	Son of Elizabeth and Zechariah, later known as John the Baptist
John	Son of Salome and Zebedee, brother of James, nephew of Mary, disciple of Jesus
Joseph	Husband of Mary, step-father of Jesus, father of James, Joseph, Judas, Simon, and three daughters
Keren	Daughter of Hirah and Miriam
King Herod	Roman-installed king of the land of Israel
Luke	Mary's interviewer, author of the Gospel of Like, traveling companion to Paul the Apostle
Magi	Astrologers from Persia, advisors to the King of Persia
Mary	Daughter of Heli and Johanna, wife of Joseph, mother of Jesus, James, Joseph, Judas, Simon, and three daughters
Matthat	Deceased husband of Abigail, father of Heli and Nahum, Mary's grandfather

List of Characters

Matthias	Son of Nahum and Esther, brother of Joel, Jessie
Micah	Innkeeper in Bethlehem, husband of Ethlan, father of Azor
Miriam	Wife of Hirah (Jerusalem merchant), mother of Keren
Nahum	Heli's brother, husband of Esther, father of Matthias, Joel, Jessie, Mary's uncle
Naphron	Food vendor in Alexandria, Egypt
Nathan	Shepherd in Bethlehem, husband of Rachel, father of Asa, Elisheba
Rabbi James	Rabbi, Nazareth synagogue
Rachel	Wife of Nathan, mother of Asa, Elisheba
Salome	Oldest daughter of Heli and Johanna, sister of Caleb, Mary, Amos, Simon; wife of Zebedee; mother of James and John (disciples of Jesus); follower of Jesus
Samuel	Johanna's father, Mary's grandfather
Simeon	Prophet at the Temple in Jerusalem
Simon	Son of Heli and Johanna, brother of Caleb, Salome, Mary, Amos
Yonatan	Resident of Nazareth, owner of olive grove
Zechariah	Husband of Elizabeth, Levitical priest, father of John (the Baptist)

CHAPTER ONE

"FAVORED"

"Mary?" Her mother's voice called through the open door as Mary stooped to plant the chickpea seeds in the just-barely-warm-enough soil. Soon it would be time to plant lentils, cucumbers, peppers, peas, lettuce, and more in the garden of their family compound. Green leaves on the grapevines and olive trees were beginning to grow, showing they were awakening from their winter slumber.

"Coming, Mama." Mary stood and shook the soil from her dress. She chided herself for not noticing earlier that the sash holding the gathered dress around her small waist had also been in the dirt. She left the bag of seeds near the garden, planning to return the next day, and brushed her hands together. Walking inside she untied the scarf that had held her long, dark, wavy hair in place while she worked in the garden and let it cascade down her back.

In the house, Johanna, her mother, was at the loom. Abigail, Johanna's mother-in-law, "Buppy" to her beloved grandchildren, was helping with the weaving. Johanna pointed to the half-finished blanket. "See how far we have progressed on making this blanket for your new home? I know the garden needs to be planted right away, but I'll have you help us on this tomorrow so you will be able to do this on your own after you and Joseph start your married life."

Mary, the Lord's Servant

"I'd love to do that, Mama," Mary replied. She smiled. Her mother was almost as excited as she was that only a few months ago at a special celebration she had been announced as Joseph's intended bride. By Jewish laws and in the eyes of the villagers, they were bound now as tightly as if married. Now they had less than a year to get everything in place to begin their life as husband and wife.

Abigail slowly stood and stretched. "I must be going home to prepare the evening meal. Caleb will be home soon." She gave Johanna and Mary each a quick peck on the cheek and started across the family compound to her house. Mary watched her cross the short distance to make sure she was safe. Abigail husband, Matthat, had died only a year ago, and it gave her comfort to have Caleb, her grandson, live within her home. Caleb, who was Johanna and Heli's oldest son and not yet married, in turn enjoyed the arrangement.

"Your papa will be home soon, too," Johanna said as her mother-in-law left, "so let's prepare tonight's meal. I asked Joseph to join us, but he is eating with Yonatan tonight. They need to discuss a project Yonatan needs for his olive grove they will start as soon as they return from Passover. Joseph said he is leaving early in the morning to go to visit his family."

Joseph had recently moved to Nazareth from Cana, just ten miles to the north, where his family lived, where he had learned the craft of a builder—shaping stones for and constructing houses, and fashioning wood into furniture, carts, yokes, handles for tools, and anything else that was requested. The iron parts of the axes, stone-cutters, and hammers were usually purchased from a Roman blacksmith—there was one in Sepphoris, currently the Roman regional capital, located between Cana and Nazareth—because Nazareth did not have a blacksmith. Joseph had come to Nazareth several times with his father, Jacob, to repair homes or their furnishings, and as he started out on his own, his father suggested

"Favored"

he make the move to Nazareth. Although Cana was a larger town, several builders lived there and Nazareth had none.

Joseph had finished his open-air shop attached to the front of his one-room house. Now that he was going to be a husband, he had started to add another room to make his home suitable for his future with Mary. His reputation preceded his move to Nazareth, and he immediately had several requests for his services. He worked on his house between building a cart for hauling grain for his friend Aaron, making the stand of a loom for Mary's Aunt Esther, and even working on a threshing sled for Mary's dad, Heli, who had mentioned he would need one soon.

Joseph wanted to finish his new room by fall so the roof could be covered with the olive pulp as Yonatan, the olive grove owner, finished the pressing of the olives from the fall's harvest that would begin in September. Joseph would prepare the roof with split poles made from pine tree trunks covered by reeds and then cover it with pulp from the olive press. As the pulp dried, the roof would be made waterproof. Yes, his new life in Nazareth was going well, especially since he and his father had approached Mary's father about a marriage bond with Mary, in Joseph's mind the prettiest and best liked girl in Nazareth. Perhaps she was why he had immediately agreed with his father's suggestion to settle here.

Nazareth was a small Jewish village with just over two hundred residents, covering only about twenty acres. Families constructed their houses close together in compounds up to an acre in size surrounded by a low rock fence; Nazareth had twelve such family compounds. Mary's family compound enclosed three houses— her family's, her Uncle Nahum's, and the original family house where her grandmother and brother lived. Nazareth also had several stand-alone houses like Joseph's.

The village was nestled in a valley inset into the top of a ridge on Mount Precipice, just north of the Jezreel Valley. At 1,300 feet above sea level, Nazareth was typically ten to twenty degrees cooler than the lower plain. Climbing at least part way up the rise to the south of Nazareth provided a good view of the Jezreel Valley and across the valley the larger city of Megiddo. On a clear day Mount Carmel (eighteen miles to the west) came into view. Beyond Mount Carmel was the Mediterranean Sea although it was obscured from view. The Jezreel Valley was fertile for grain crops—barley and wheat. Some less affluent farmers, like Mary's father, had cleared rocks and planted crops on a few acres of land near Nazareth on the more gentle slopes of Mount Precipice and on to the north, using the stones as low fences to deter sheep. Other areas remained rocky and were grazing fields for the flocks of sheep dotting the slopes. A few olive groves, an orange grove, and one large vineyard were also near the town. Across the path from Mary's family compound was a two-acre field where the village residents kept their working animals, currently two oxen and several donkeys.

To the east of Nazareth, but out of view, was Mount Tabor and beyond that, the Jordan River spilled out of the Sea of Galilee, sixteen miles to the east. Villages dotted the shore of the eight-by-fifteen-mile Sea. A Roman city, Tiberias, was being built on the west shore of the Sea of Galilee to later become the Roman regional capital. Often builders like Jacob and Joseph were summoned to do work there. Roman soldiers occasionally rode through Nazareth to make their presence and domination of the area known.

Joseph stood up and admired the first almost-completed wall of his house's second room. He couldn't see Mary's parents' house from his, but he knew Mary was also excited about preparing all that she would bring into the home.

Mary washed her hands with the little bit of water left in the washing jar and mentioned to her mother that more water would be needed when her father returned home. "Will you watch the boys while I go to the spring to fill the small jar with water?" Johanna asked.

"Favored"

"Yes, of course." Mary knew that meant keeping her eight- and ten-year-old brothers from running through the freshly planted garden as they played with their two cousins who lived next door. She was planning to direct all of them to help her finish planting the seeds within a few days. All four boys had already spent the morning and early afternoon at the synagogue learning Hebrew, studying the Laws and the Prophets along with Israel's history, as was required of all boys, and spent the late afternoon running off their pent-up energy.

Mary's mother picked up the gallon-sized, wide-mouth jar and started toward the path. "No, wait," she said. She stopped and turned around. "Would you go get the water while I start the lentil soup?" This seemed like the better plan.

Oh, yes! Mary would much rather go get the water. Her mother handed her the water jar, and she happily headed out of the yard. She turned right, taking the main road through the town, knowing this route would take her past Joseph's house.

As she walked just beyond their family compound, she waved and called greetings to her best friend, Hannah, who was helping her mother gather up the last of their fresh laundry from the drying tree. A little further and quite a few yards back from the road, she saw Joseph stretching after placing another stone on the wall and filling in with the masonry compound. He didn't see her, but she was not allowed to be with him unless another adult was with her, so she just smiled at his back and went on.

The spring on the edge of the village bubbled from a rock formation and splashed into a deep pool. Mary always paused there for a few moments to listen to its soothing, gurgling sounds. Usually others would be at the spring filling water jars, and they would exchange greetings, but this time no one was there. Mary used the rope to pull up the bucket to fill her water jar, and then placed it on her shoulder, steadying it as she held to its handle. She reminded herself she needed to make a similar jar for her future home the

Mary, the Lord's Servant

next time the village kiln was heated for use. Happy thoughts of God's blessings to her filled her mind as she headed back home. She opted to take the shorter, but narrower and hillier path back home. It would take her up and over the rise behind her family's compound.

Just before she turned the corner toward her house, an angel in bright white clothing appeared suddenly in the path. Startled and frightened, Mary nearly dropped the water jar, spilling half of its contents on the ground. She managed to set it down as she collapsed onto a large rock.

The angel spoke to her, "Greetings, favored woman! The Lord is with you." Mary's heart was pounding, her eyes wide with fright. She held her breath, her mind racing to understand WHAT is this?! The angel calmed her, "Don't be afraid, Mary, for you have found favor with God! You will conceive and give birth to a son, and you will name him Jesus. He will be very great and will be called the Son of the Most High. The Lord God will give him the throne of his ancestor David. And he will reign over Israel forever; his Kingdom will never end!"

Mary knew the angel was speaking of the Messiah — the long-promised Messiah! Every Sabbath in their village synagogue, everyone prayed that the Messiah would come. The angel was saying HE IS COMING NOW ... as a baby ... she would be his mother ... But how? She and Joseph were not yet united as husband and wife, yet this angel was indicating RIGHT NOW. Mary was so frightened, so dumbstruck, she wasn't sure her voice would work, but it did. She asked the angel, "But how can this happen? I am a virgin."

The angel explained, "The Holy Spirit will come upon you, and the power of the Most High will overshadow you. So the baby to be born will be holy, and he will be called the Son of God. What's more, your relative Elizabeth has become pregnant in her old age!

People used to say she was barren, but she has conceived a son and is now in her sixth month. For nothing is impossible with God."

Elizabeth? With child? Her mother's cousin? In her 60s! With child? God can do anything!

In awe, Mary humbly whispered, "I am the Lord's servant. May everything you have said about me come true." And then the angel left her.

Mary was shaken to her core. Had she just seen a vision or was that angel real? YES, he was! What should she do? She looked around and down the dirt path. No one was within sight. She didn't know how long she sat there taking in several deep breaths. Her hands were still shaking as she picked up the now half-filled water jar and her legs were a bit wobbly as she continued toward home.

As Mary entered the yard, her mother was stirring the soup in the covered, outdoor kitchen and didn't look up at first. "What took you—?" She dropped the rest of her question after a quick glance at Mary's pale face and let go of the wooden stirring spoon. "Are you okay? What happened? Come inside and sit down."

The boys were not within earshot, so Mary tried to find her voice.

"Mama, I ... I saw an angel," she managed to say as she sank into the nearest chair.

Her mother's eyes widened, and she put her hand over her mouth as she drew in a breath. "What?! Tell me all about it." All else was forgotten as Mary shakily told her mother what the angel had said. Somewhere in Mary's telling, her mother collapsed on another chair. Tears began streaming from her eyes. Mary joined her in her tears, from amazement, from answered prayers, from the unknown that was ahead, and from spilled-over shock. Yes, everyone was praying, pleading in their prayers for the Messiah to come. Now, Johanna's daughter had been chosen to give birth to the Messiah! The angel twice had said God "favored" her! Yes, Mary's father was of the tribe of Judah, of royal lineage, a descendant of David, but for God to choose Mary was ... was, oh, unfathomable!

Mary, the Lord's Servant

Then suddenly questions spilled out of both of them ... What about Joseph? Was God really going to "overshadow" Mary and she would be with child ... without a husband? Where would she live? Would she be subject to stoning for being an unwed mother? Would God confirm this announcement to them?

Yes, they suddenly realized, He already had. The angel said that Elizabeth is pregnant. Johanna's cousin was much older than she was and had always prayed for a child. But she was barren, a "curse" among all the tribes, a presumed sign of God's disfavor. But the angel had said that Elizabeth was with child — and in her sixth month! Was it true? Why hadn't Elizabeth sent word to Johanna, her much-loved cousin? Was this God's way of confirming to them that they could trust the rest of what had been announced to Mary?

Mary and Johanna had the same thought at the same time and said it almost together — Mary should go to Elizabeth's house to confirm that she indeed was with child, then they could confidently cling to the other promises in the angel's message. But how? They would need to convince Mary's father, Heli, that she should accompany him to Passover. He was leaving in less than two days. Some of the village men who walked slowly had already left to travel the seventy miles to Jerusalem. Since his crop of winter wheat wouldn't be ready for harvest for several weeks, today Heli was helping his brother Nahum with his flock of sheep as a few of the ewes were giving birth. Caleb, Heli's oldest son, worked with his uncle Nahum because he wanted to learn all he could about being a shepherd before beginning his own flock. He preferred caring for sheep over tilling the soil as his father did. Caleb, too, would be going to Passover and his uncle's flock would be left in the care of the hired hands. Heli would be home soon; the sky showed the sun had almost set beyond the hill to the west. Surely they would be able to convince him that Mary should go along and visit Elizabeth. She would have to hurry to get ready but ... .

"Favored"

Just then Heli came in the door followed by the boys loudly announcing, "Papa's home!" Even in the darkening room Heli could see the tear-stained, yet smiling faces of his wife and youngest daughter. The lentil soup was a bit past done, but nothing else had been prepared for their evening meal. His question, "What's the mat—?" was interrupted as Mary jumped up and ran to him, giving him a hug, crying, "Oh, Papa."

"Is it time to eat?" the boys asked in unison.

"Amos, Simon, go wash for the meal," Johanna instructed. "We need to say a few words to your papa."

How could Mary and Johanna possibly explain what had happened in "a few words"? Mary said the same first words she had said to her mother: "I saw an angel." But Heli's reaction was not like his wife's had been.

He needed a quick summary. "Is this good or bad news?" he wanted to know. "The boys will be back in here in seconds."

"Good," Mary smiled.

"Maybe both," Johanna said, as the boys ran back into the room, hands still dripping wet.

Heli quietly instructed, "First, Mary, light a lamp while I go wash, then help your mother finish preparing for the evening meal. Boys, be seated." Then he looked from his wife to his daughter. "This discussion will wait until after we eat."

His reaction almost frightened Mary. He was too composed. Didn't he believe her? How could he so calmly sit and eat with this suspended announcement?

The evening meal was simple; the lentil soup was the main portion of this meal. Johanna added some hummus to spread on the last of the dried flatbread, olives, and some dried fruit from the fall harvest. Heli gave the blessing and the meal proceeded in the usual manner. The boys answered questions from their father regarding their studies at the synagogue. Finally, Heli told the boys to play outside for just a short time so he could talk with his wife

Mary, the Lord's Servant

and daughter. It was almost completely dark, but the boys could always find ways to occupy themselves outside.

Heli gave his full attention to Mary as she relived those amazing moments and told him clearly what the angel had said. She didn't add anything to the angel's message but repeated it verbatim because it was indelibly etched in her mind. Heli's face showed he was soaking it all in with amazement. Johanna started to interject further thoughts, but Heli held up his hand and said, "I need to think and pray. Put the boys to bed. I'll let you know when I have something to say."

Heli was a good and righteous man. He knew how fervently everyone prayed for the promised Messiah to come. Surely the Roman oppressors would be no match for the conquering Messiah announced in the Scriptures. The stunned father's first thoughts were about Mary, his beloved Mary. She was such a good and humble girl, never giving him any reason to correct her, eager to also know the will of the God of Israel. She wouldn't be making this up, would she? NO, she wouldn't! What about Joseph? Heli had been so pleased that if he had to part with Mary at least she was going to be the wife of one who also fervently worshiped God and lived what he believed.

"O God of Abraham, Isaac, and Jacob, please guide my thoughts and actions," Heli pled. It had been his prayer many times, but now more than ever he needed to know what God wanted him to do. For a few moments his mind was overwhelmed with everything all at once, and he could focus on nothing specifically. He forced other things out of mind and carefully reviewed what Mary had told him about the angel's message: ". . . favored woman ... the Lord is with you ... You will give birth to a son ... the Son of the Most High ... the throne of his ancestor David ... the Holy Spirit will come ... the power of the Most High will overshadow you." And Mary had humbly accepted the angel's message, saying, "I am the Lord's servant."

"Favored"

He pondered the fact that Mary, in that holy, yet frightening moment was willing to do as God asked. She had a choice, and she chose to obey. Heli then remembered Mary had said the angel also announced, ". . . Elizabeth has become pregnant ... and is in her sixth month." He finally concluded: I must go visit Elizabeth and Zechariah after I go to Passover in Jerusalem, not to question Mary's words but to confirm what God told Mary through the angel. A second thought came to him: Mary will want to go herself. It would be good for her to talk with Elizabeth. But should she go? Could she go? Three days of walking, many hours each day. All men were required to go to Passover; some women accompanied their husbands, especially when a son celebrated his coming of age, and often entire families traveled there. Johanna was not going this year. She had already agreed to care for Nahum's two younger children since Nahum's son Matthias had turned twelve years old and had finished his studies at the synagogue. Nahum and Esther, his wife, and Matthias were traveling with the group leaving the day after tomorrow, as were Heli and Caleb. Could Mary be prepared to go in that time?

Heli left his prayer spot and returned to the house's main room. Johanna and Mary were huddled together, praying. They heard him come into the room and looked up.

"Mary, my child," Heli hesitated. He would never again be able to think of Mary as his precious little girl. She had suddenly grown up in his eyes into a woman, a woman God had chosen to bring the Messiah into the world. "Mary," he sighed and started again, "this is an amazing thing, so very hard to fathom. I believe you and I believe God knows you to be the perfect one to bring the Messiah into the world. Let me say again, I believe you, but I do think that God wants me ... perhaps you ... to confirm His message to you by visiting Elizabeth. If she is indeed with child and is in her sixth month—exactly as the angel said—then we can know that all the

Mary, the Lord's Servant

rest of what the angel announced will come to pass exactly as the angel said."

"Oh, Papa," Mary voice broke as sudden tears of relief flooded her eyes since her father had come to the same conclusion as she and her mother had. "May I go to Elizabeth? Yes, I know it will be hard, but I know I can do it. Mama, can you do without me in caring for the four boys while Papa and I are gone?" As the oldest daughter now in the home since her sister, Salome, was married, Mary was concerned for her mother.

"Yes, of course," Johanna smiled. "And Buppy will be here, too. This is the best way for you to know. Elizabeth is a wonderful woman of God. She will be so excited to see you. And she will help you understand Scriptures about the Messiah. Oh, yes, you must go."

Heli knew in his heart this was the right decision, but he also understood the difficulties and obstacles of taking Mary with him to Passover and then five miles west to Ein Kerem, where Zechariah and Elizabeth lived. For now, they needed to discuss details of the pilgrimage, leaving in only thirty-six hours. He knew Esther would gladly help him keep an eye on Mary.

"BUT," Heli strongly cautioned, "no one must know why Mary is going with me to Jerusalem and then on to Ein Kerem, except to say that she is visiting her cousin. Mary, you must tell no one in Nazareth about the angel's visit until after your return, not even Joseph. He is leaving early in the morning to walk to Cana to travel to Passover with his family for the last time before … ." He had started to say ". . . before you are married," but now he was concerned as to what Joseph's reaction would be. So much prayer was needed for the Lord's guidance!

Heli continued, "You, too, Johanna. Tell no one, not even our other children. God has this in His hands and we will allow Him to direct us in all things." Both women acknowledged their agreement, even though something this marvelous would be difficult to keep

"Favored"

inside. Then, past their usual bedtime, Mary and Johanna began to plan how to prepare Mary for the journey.

Just before Heli retired to bed, Mary asked him, "How long may I stay with Elizabeth?"

Heli thought a moment. "Well, that week of the Passover and Feast of Unleavened Bread celebration is probably not long enough. I won't be in Jerusalem again until the Feast of Pentecost, Mary. Elizabeth would want you to stay that long and probably could use your help for those seven weeks. You will need to come home with me then."

Mary and her mother talked long into the night and went to bed only because the lamp had burned all its oil. By the time they laid their heads down to sleep, they had discussed all the possibilities, hopefully, of travel preparations, extra food and clothing. Of course the discussion came around to Mary having a baby. No, not just a baby, but the long awaited Messiah. Oh, what did the future hold?

CHAPTER TWO

TRAVEL DAYS

Mary's sleep didn't come for quite some time. Her mind played the angel's visit over and over again. She was amazed, excited, nervous, astounded—all at once. Would she ever sleep? But as the sun arose, so did she. One day! She had one day to get ready.

Heli again cautioned Johanna and Mary about keeping the angel's visit and message to themselves, saying only that Mary's sudden desire to go was to visit her cousin Elizabeth. He then went next door to meet up with his son Caleb so the two could join Nahum and his flock. Nahum and his son Matthias had stayed in the field overnight, but they were close to the village. Heli would notify his mother and Caleb and then Nahum of Mary's plans to join the travel group.

Johanna went next door to Nahum's house to let Esther know Mary had decided to visit her cousin Elizabeth in Ein Kerem. When Esther reacted with great surprise, Johanna changed the conversation to the day's work. Mary's clothes would need to be washed and hung to dry. The hearth oven in the middle of the compound would need to be cleaned first for baking the Passover bread, and then the fire started under the oven. Finally both batches of the bread dough would be prepared for baking. As they discussed these duties, they had walked to Johanna's house, "Buppy" Abigail had joined them, and the work was divided among the four women.

Mary and her mother washed both her everyday dress and her Sabbath day dress while she wore her mother's worn-out dress. After today it would be used for rags or cut up and the good parts re-used for a child's garment. Mary's sandals, with their reed soles (currently her only shoes), would probably — they must! — get her there and back.

While spreading her dresses out to dry, Mary glanced toward the garden and remembered what she had planned to do in the days ahead. She turned to her mother. "Oh, Mama, what about the garden?"

Johanna chuckled. "The boys and I will plant it, probably not quite as well as if you were supervising, but we will get it planted. And if it doesn't rain soon, we will carry water from the spring."

The weekly baking day had been changed in order to make an adequate supply of bread for those traveling to Passover. Fresh bread was enjoyed the first two or three days after a baking day, but the remaining bread supply was baked as flatbread and dried in the sun to prevent spoilage. That bread was eaten by dipping it in a liquid — perhaps water, olive oil, wine or fruit juice, depending on what was available — or eaten crisp with a topping such as hummus. The dry flatbread was best for travel. On this baking day the Passover bread, made without yeast, was to be baked first.

First, the wheat for the breads was ground as fine as they could grind it by hand using the small, concave limestone rock and the hand held grinding stone. It would take more than an hour of work to produce an adequate amount of wheat flour. While Johanna and Mary worked at grinding the wheat, Abigail helped Esther as she scrubbed the oven clean.

Using a flint stone, Abigail and Mary started the fire in the hearth under the oven. Waiting to make sure the fire was taking hold, Mary's grandmother remarked, "You didn't mention yesterday that

Travel Days

you wanted to go see Elizabeth, Mary." She looked lovingly at Mary and asked her, "Are you sure you want to go?"

"Oh, yes, Buppy," Mary said enthusiastically. "I so very much want to spend some time with Elizabeth ..." she hesitated and added, "before I am married."

"Then let's make sure you get ready today!" Abigail said as they joined Johanna and Esther inside the house.

Encouraged by her mother-in-law's approval of Mary's travel, Esther offered, "Since we are taking our hand cart, I'm sure there will be plenty of space in our cart for Mary's things."

Mary smiled at her aunt and said, "Thank you! That will be helpful."

Johanna and Esther finished mixing the bread dough containing yeast and Mary placed it in a covered dish outside the house. Then the rest of the yeast was removed from the home, in accordance with the Law. Johanna and Esther thoroughly washed the preparing table to remove all traces of yeast before beginning to mix the Passover bread dough. As soon as it was ready, the Passover bread was placed in the now-hot oven.

They were soon joined by Hannah, her mother, and two other families, each bringing their bread dough to bake. The women enjoyed each other's company on baking day.

There were only four ovens in the village and families shared the hot ovens because of the limited supply of wood to burn. Nahum, Caleb, and other shepherds would gather sticks found in the fields as they cared for the flocks. The families saved trimmings of olive trees and other trees, dead trees that had been chopped down, and even Joseph's wood chippings. Nothing was wasted.

Immediately Hannah's gaze went from Mary, who was wearing her mother's worn-out dress, to Mary's freshly washed dresses spread out to dry. Seeing the questioning look in Hannah's eyes, Mary stated simply, "Mama and I have decided I should travel with the others to Jerusalem tomorrow and then go on to Ein Kerem to visit our cousin Elizabeth."

With her long dark hair and similar soft facial features, Hannah could have passed for Mary's sister even though she was almost a head taller. She knew her friend too well to let her statement go uncontested. Confronting Mary, she said accusingly, "You haven't mentioned this before. Why the sudden decision to go?"

"Mama and I talked about it, and Papa agreed last night that if I could get ready in one day I should go," Mary replied as nonchalantly as possible.

Hannah's mother, a bit of a busybody, was quick to chime in. "But Mary, you should stay here to prepare for your upcoming marriage. What did Joseph have to say about this?"

Mary blushed a bit, hoping it didn't show. "He left early this morning for Cana to travel with his family to Jerusalem," she stated almost too casually. "It means walking extra miles but he wanted to honor his father in this way. Since our family didn't make our final decision until last night, we had no time to speak with Joseph."

"Mary will have plenty of time to finish marriage preparations after she returns," Johanna hastily added. "Oh, look, Abigail. Our Passover bread is done and we need to get it out of the oven so the others can use it." As Johanna removed the bread from the oven using a large, flat spatula, she instructed, "Mary, go ahead and take this into the house."

Holding a folded woolen cloth for protection, Mary took the loaf, and Abigail offered, "I'll take the other one."

Abigail followed Mary into the house. As the women placed the hot bread on the cooling racks, Abigail remarked. "Hannah is rather upset with you, Mary. But I must say your mother's old dress looks terrible on you." They laughed together as they returned to the others gathered around the oven in the yard. Buppy gave Mary a quick hug.

Travel Days

Then to turn the conversation in another direction, Mary said to her mother, "Please tell me again how you and Papa met. I know the story, but I need to hear it again."

Johanna laughed out loud. The other ladies wanted to hear the story, too. "Yes, Mary, you have heard the story, but I love telling it."

She looked around at the women waiting to hear her story and began: "I had just turned fourteen," she turned to Mary, "like you are now and begged my father, Samuel, to take me to Jerusalem for the festivities of the Feast of Tabernacles." She had told the women in the past that her mother died in childbirth when Johanna was ten years old. "He didn't have time to look after me as he had too many priestly duties," Johanna continued, "but Elizabeth, wonderful Elizabeth said she would be responsible for me. She was already married to Zechariah; he would not be on duty as a Levitical priest that day so we traveled together from Ein Kerem to Jerusalem. We were in the market — you know how crowded it gets — and we could hardly get through the narrow street. We stopped in a shop where Elizabeth bought a lovely shawl for me. Zechariah gladly allowed Elizabeth to buy things for me like they would have for a child if they had one."

Johanna hesitated again, smiled almost to herself, and then looked at Mary. "Elizabeth and I were still looking at the beautiful fabrics with the merchant when Zechariah was introduced to your Papa and his father, Matthat, through a mutual acquaintance right there in that busy market. After purchasing the scarf, we had just headed out to meet up with Zechariah when I saw him talking to your papa. I think I loved him from that moment I first saw him. He was handsome and shy and just barely smiled at me. Shortly after that, the next time we were in Jerusalem for a festival, your grandfather Matthat approached my father through Zechariah to secure a marriage bond. I know it is unusual that such a meeting between someone from the tribe of Judah and someone from the tribe of Levi would make a marriage bond. But I think Zechariah is

Mary, the Lord's Servant

a romantic, and he saw the stars in my eyes and suggested it would be a good marriage. And it is. I miss being close to my family very much, especially Elizabeth, since my father is gone now too, but I love your Papa. He is a wonderful man of God and does all he can to provide for us. We aren't rich, but we enjoy the love of our family and friends." She indicated those gathered around her.

The women all enjoyed the story. Soon they were telling the stories of their families and the baking time went by quickly.

The sun was high in the sky when the first of the flatbread was to be placed on the drying racks in the sun. The sun would dry and preserve the bread to delay spoilage. The challenge now was to make sure the birds didn't come have a feast, so Mary and Hannah were assigned to sit near the outdoor drying racks to protect the bread.

Still clearly upset with her friend, Hannah took the opportunity to once again ask, "Why didn't you tell me you were thinking of going?" Hannah was a year younger than Mary, and she and Mary had shared all their secrets since they were very young. Hannah disliked that she had been left out of this discussion and decision.

"I ... we decided only a few hours ago that I must go spend some time with my cousin Elizabeth. Papa says I can stay there until he returns to Jerusalem, but I am anxious to get other things done for my marriage when I get back. And I still want you to help me, like we discussed." Mary tried to be more positive than she felt at that moment.

"What will Joseph say when he finds out?" Hannah asked.

"Papa will take me to Elizabeth's before Passover. If we see Joseph ... yes, it will be a surprise to him. Don't worry, Hannah, everything will work out fine," Mary said, trying to reassure her friend that it was unnecessary for her be concerned about Mary's sudden shift in plans. Mary again changed the subject by asking Hannah about her feelings for the village young men, especially Caleb. She knew Hannah had her eye on Caleb, and it was at least

Travel Days

possible that some day Hannah might be her sister-in-law although Caleb wanted to get his flock established before he made that step.

By mid-afternoon all the bread was baked, the fire had died, and the yard was cleared of the bakers. The boys had returned from the synagogue, happy they had two weeks without schooling as Rabbi James would be gone to Passover and the week-long Feast of Unleavened Bread. Knowing the boys' activity in the yard would keep the birds away from the almost dried bread, Mary and Johanna were able to go inside to finish gathering more dried fruit and nuts for the trip. They retrieved some fresh fruit along with a filled wine skin for the Passover celebration from the cool, limestone storage well. They wrapped the flatbread for the journey separate from the Passover bread since the two breads were not to be mingled.

Mary did not know Elizabeth as well as her mother did, of course, but felt the same love for her that Johanna had. It had been four years since she had spent time with Elizabeth. Four years earlier, Heli had taken his entire family to Jerusalem as Caleb completed his studies at the synagogue and they all had gone to celebrate together during Passover.

That had been a memorable trip. Heli showed his love for his wife by arranging that after the festivities in Jerusalem the family would spend a week with Elizabeth and Zechariah in Ein Kerem. What a joy it had been to get to know her mother's cousin and to witness the love between the much older Elizabeth and Johanna. Age didn't seem to matter. They were family. Elizabeth loved getting to know all of Johanna's children, but Mary did note a tinge of sadness in Elizabeth's eyes as she watched the younger ones playing in the courtyard of Zechariah and Elizabeth's rather elaborate home. It was much fancier than the plain houses in Nazareth. But this was the house of a priest and his stature in the community was reflected in their home. Elizabeth had even hired a second servant to help her maid Carmen with the family of seven that visited for a week. But after that week, they knew they needed to head back to Jerusalem to connect with another group of travelers heading back north. Travelers walked in groups to be safe from those who would prey on lone travelers and from wild animals that roamed the Judean Wilderness, which stretched sixty miles along the Dead Sea and north into the Jordan River Valley.

Mary sighed as she thought of the trip ahead of them. She definitely was excited about going to see Elizabeth to prove the angel's words were true, but preparing to travel in one day was exhausting! The busy day sped by quickly, too quickly. They all fell onto their sleeping mats very tired but satisfied with all they had accomplished.

At dawn, travelers made their final preparations and said farewells to family members and friends who were not going to Passover. Just before Mary left the house, her mother quietly pressed two copper shekels into her hand. Mary was surprised. "This is all I can spare, Mary, but you may need it," Mama said, "perhaps to buy some new sandal straps if you must. Your Papa has extra money for food in Jerusalem. I will constantly pray for you. Please greet Elizabeth on my behalf and help her in any way you can. Remember God is watching over you."

They paused, hugged, and Mary tearfully hurried out the door to catch up with her father. It would not be good to be late to the meeting place on this first morning of their journey. Johanna experienced a jumble of emotions as she watched Mary practically run down the path. She wanted to sit down and cry, but just then Nahum and Esther's two youngest sons, Joel and Jessie, noisily greeted their cousins. Johanna sighed. The next several days were going to be a challenge.

The six from Mary's family—Heli and Mary, Nahum and Esther, and Caleb and Matthias— merged with the group of Nazareth travelers. Expressions of surprise to see Mary joining them spread quickly among those who had not yet heard. Hannah was there

Travel Days

to see her father off and gave Mary a quick hug. Nonetheless, she still clearly questioned Mary's motives for her sudden decision without having previously mentioned it to her. "I will tell you all about my visit when I get back, Hannah," Mary told her as she moved with the others heading down the road toward the Jezreel Valley. Mary heard an elder of the village call, "Let us go to the house of the Lord!"

Nahum pulled the small cart that held the food items including the Passover bread and wine, clothing, and other essentials for the six from their family. Heli would take several turns in pulling the cart. They had also informed the boys that they would do some of the work of pulling the cart. But as they started, Caleb and Matthias were already at the front of the group, anxious to get the trip under way.

So the long trek began. Travelers from the Nazareth area took the safest, although longest, route to Jerusalem, which took them along the Jordan River. The shorter route went through Samaria but the Jews from Galilee weren't always welcomed in Samaria, especially when traveling to Passover. The group from Nazareth would go east through the Jezreel Valley to connect to the north-south road along the Jordan River that merchants also used. At this time of year the road was packed with many people, mostly those going to Passover, but also a few caravans with goods to sell in all the towns along the way and especially in Jerusalem.

The goal of those going to Passover was to walk at least twenty-five miles the first day, the easiest day of travel. They would camp together for safety each night. The second day's travel would take them into the Judean Wilderness, an area of more hills, bleaker scenery and warmer weather. By the second day's end they hoped their camp would be near Jericho, which was only twenty miles from Jerusalem but much lower in elevation. The third day's travel promised to be exciting as they neared Jerusalem. From Jericho, they would turn west toward tall hills, the route that would take

Mary, the Lord's Servant

them into the Holy City. On that day, the travelers would sing many of David's psalms, Songs of Ascent, as they climbed the hills; the final hill was the Mount of Olives. As they reached its peak, the view that greeted them would make all the effort, tired feet, and sore muscles worthwhile! The view of Jerusalem and the Temple of God! Nothing compared to that moment!

As they reached the Jezreel Valley floor, the band from Nazareth admired the golden fields of barley, soon to be harvested. The wheat fields in the distance were losing the green immature color as they began to ripen. On this first day, Mary walked beside Esther and talked easily with her aunt. At first Esther tried again to probe Mary about her sudden decision to visit her cousin; Mary was able to answer her satisfactorily without revealing the news about the angel's visit.

Mary smiled with Esther as they heard her uncle Nahum quizzing his son Matthias, now walking with the family group. Matthias had passed all the exams by the rabbi at the synagogue, but now he honored his father by proving he deserved the "completion of studies" honors. *What is that mount to the west?* Mt. Carmel. *What happened there?* Elijah defeated the prophets of Baal. *What happened over there by Megiddo?* King Josiah died in battle, and before that it was one of King Solomon's regional capitals.

Mary knew that soon Matthias would identify the Jordan River, where further to the south the children of Israel crossed into the land promised by God. Later the Syrian commander Naaman had obediently dipped in the muddy Jordan River and God healed him of leprosy. They passed near the springs where Gideon's soldiers refreshed themselves before God's miracle of defeating 135,000 Midianite soldiers with only three hundred Israeli soldiers. Coming into view was the tall hill called Mount Gilboa where King Saul and his three sons died in battle. By noon the travelers were nearing the large Roman city of Scythopolis, known in King Saul's time as Beth Shan. At that time it was a Philistine city where the bodies of Saul and his sons had been hung by the Philistines on the city wall. Israeli soldiers had bravely removed the bodies under cover of night so they could be properly buried. It was a walking history lesson, one that Mary loved hearing. Although she wasn't allowed to attend the school at the synagogue, her brothers had discussed many of their lessons with their father at home. Mary loved the history of her people and stories of God's provision, intervention, and promises.

Near Scythopolis the Nazareth travelers stopped for a brief rest and a bit of food. Mary's father had frequently glanced at her with concern, and he was grateful when the group decided to take a rest. Shortly, they were again on their way, urged on by the young people of the group. The congestion on the road lessened after passing the city as many of the merchant caravans had stopped to sell their wares to the Romans there.

Esther and Mary visited about Mary's plans for preparing for her upcoming marriage ceremony, including making bedding and using the kiln to make kitchenware and lamps. There was something guarded in Mary's voice, but Esther knew Mary was already somewhat tired and there were many miles ahead.

The men, including Rabbi James, took the opportunity of these days together to talk about the Word of God: the Law of Moses, the Psalms, the Prophets, and of course the talk came around to the prophecies about the coming Messiah. They discussed several passages that the rabbi had recently read in the Prophets and mentioned David's references in the Psalms. There was disagreement whether some of the passages pertained to the Messiah, but all agreed that they were anxious for the Messiah to come. Heli joined in the discussion but this time paid closer attention to all that was said. Finally they all agreed when Heli concluded, "God will reveal all that we need to know when we need to know it."

The weather was good and their spirits high; at day's end they stopped for the night, having gone even further than anticipated.

Mary, the Lord's Servant

Finding soft ground for sleeping was not easy, and each person had to move several rocks as they all settled down for the night. Mary was tired — oh, so tired — but she was probably no more tired than anyone else. Even on the hard ground, she fell asleep quickly wrapped in the warm, wool blanket her mother had insisted she bring. The men took turns staying awake during the night hours to guard the rest of the sleeping travelers from the night's dangers.

As the sky started growing lighter, Mary awakened to the voices of families stirring and men singing their morning prayers together. As they ate their breakfast of bread, dried fruit, nuts, and some apples and oranges from the fall harvest, the sun made its appearance over the low mountains to the east of the Jordan River. They filled their water skins for the day's journey from a nearby stream where the water was clear before it flowed into the Jordan. They started toward Jerusalem once again.

Yes, that day the scenery changed. The hills became more barren. By late morning only small patches of grasses and some scraggly bushes covered the brown ground. The group of travelers did occasionally see a flock of sheep in the distance, but very few people lived in these barren hills. Only the Jordan River bank displayed any greenery, except for the infrequent wadis that had been dug by the rare downpours of rain. Even the trees along the river were scrawnier in this area than closer to the Sea of Galilee. Occasionally the travelers stopped for a short rest, but they couldn't rest much because the sun was warm even in late March. So they mostly kept moving along although Mary gratefully noticed the pace was a bit slower. Their goal was to camp near Jericho at night.

The highlight of the day was when a merchant of palm dates caught up with them and offered the travelers a taste of his wares. He didn't charge much and almost everyone purchased a supply and was refreshed by the deliciously sweet fruit. His palm grove was near Jericho, where he would refill his supply to sell in Jerusalem. Mary hoped they could buy more when they reached Jerusalem.

Travel Days

Finally Mary was relieved to hear someone say, "We're almost to our overnight stop. Please keep up the pace. Soon we can rest for the night."

Mary was more than ready to stop and almost too weary to eat, but she knew she couldn't let her father or especially her aunt know that she was quite tired, so she ate the offered food — the same flatbread, fruit, and nuts — and found a place near her father, aunt and uncle to lie down. Her father asked in a quiet voice, "Are you doing all right?"

"Oh, yes, Papa," Mary sighed, "but I am tired and ready for sleep." And she was sound asleep almost before she finished answering. She dreamed of desert camels, spices she had smelled as the merchants passed by, and Joseph giving her a palm date. *How did he get into my dream?* she wondered as she awoke.

The final day of travel faced them: a shorter distance but much more difficult. The road ahead was similar to climbing from the Jezreel Valley to the top of Mount Precipice three times in one day. "Take a deep breath and do it, Mary," she challenged herself.

Early morning praises filled the air—theirs and other pilgrims' who were going to Jerusalem. They joined together in singing:

> I was glad when they said to me, "Let us go to the house of the Lord."
> And now here we are, standing inside your gates, O Jerusalem.
> Jerusalem is a well-built city; its seamless walls cannot be breached.
> All the tribes of Israel — the Lord's people — make their pilgrimage here.
> They come to give thanks to the name of the Lord, as the law requires of Israel.
> Here stand the thrones where judgment is given, the thrones of the dynasty of David.

Mary, the Lord's Servant

> Pray for peace in Jerusalem. May all those who love this
> city prosper.
> O Jerusalem, may there be peace within your walls and
> prosperity in your palaces.
> For the sake of my family and friends, I will say, "May
> you have peace."
> For the sake of the house of the Lord our God,
> I will seek what is best for you, O Jerusalem.

The travelers sang often with intervals of quiet meditation as they walked up the hills toward Jerusalem.

> I look up to the mountains—
> does my help come from there?
> My help comes from the Lord, who made heaven
> and earth.
> He will not let you stumble;
> the one who watches over you will not slumber;
> Indeed, he who watches over Israel never slumbers
> or sleeps.
> The Lord himself watches over you!
> The Lord stands beside you as your protective shade.
> The sun will not harm you by day, nor the moon
> at night.
> The Lord keeps you from all harm and watches over
> your life.
> The Lord keeps watch over you as you come and go,
> both now and forever.

The climb was difficult, seemingly endless, but Mary was determined to enjoy these final twenty miles. Finally, as the sun began to dip toward the western horizon and the travelers crowded the road as it climbed the eastern slope of the Mount of Olives, they reached the top. The amazing scene of Jerusalem and the Temple of God came into view — the tall stone walls of Jerusalem, the hundreds of visitors spilling out of the Golden Gate, and especially the Temple of the Lord gleaming in the setting sun. King Herod, even though he was a cruel ruler, had been used by God to wonderfully enlarge the Temple grounds and enhance the Temple with new marble stones and a large amount of gold overlay. The building project was well underway.

Hearts swelled with joy as the weary tribe looked at the sight in front of them. The smoke from the evening sacrifices hung above the Temple, then fanned out in the winds above. The group from Nazareth wanted to spend time just soaking in the view and atmosphere, but the setting sun urged them to descend the Mount of Olives toward the north, as they had previously planned, to a campsite on the northern slopes in an olive grove. They would spend the night here and have one day to rest before the Passover began with the evening sacrifice the next evening. Hundreds of thousands of pilgrims had come together to celebrate how God had saved their ancestors from the bondage of slavery in Egypt to bring them into this their Promised Land. Today campsites surrounded the city of Jerusalem. What a marvelous time they would have here!

CHAPTER THREE

WITH ELIZABETH

Mary slept even with achy feet, achy back, achy everything. It seemed she had slept only a short time when her father touched her shoulder. "Mary, come, get up. Let us be going to Ein Kerem so I can get back before Passover begins. Nahum will buy and prepare the Passover lamb for our family. I want you to rest in a real bed tonight."

A real bed. That sounded so good to Mary's sleepy mind. So she arose, noting the pink sky. They prepared to walk through Jerusalem and then the almost five miles beyond the other side of Jerusalem westward to Ein Kerem. Because of the chill of the morning, she draped her blanket around her shoulders, and her father helped her secure it with the rope normally used to make it into a back bundle. She folded her Sabbath dress to carry. She would see Elizabeth today! By the time they reached the city walls, the sun had peaked over the Mount of Olives.

They entered the city at the Sheep Gate, just north of the Temple area, and walked through the northern portions of the city then south toward the Gennath (Jaffa) Gate, just north of Herod's Palace grounds. Mary noticed the stark difference between the large, two-story houses of the rich — government officers, priests and elite religious leaders, merchants — and the small one-story houses of residents of less means that were crowded together. Even in

Mary, the Lord's Servant

this early morning hour the city was teeming with people moving from one place to another. Merchants were beginning to open their shops. The delightful smells of food cooking enticed father and daughter to stop, but they were determined to get to their destination. Because of the crowded streets, it took them longer than they had expected to get through the city, which was so very much larger than tiny Nazareth. Mary also noticed the presence of many Roman soldiers, many of them on horses, forcing their way through the groups of pilgrims.

On the other side of Jerusalem, travelers walked toward the Holy City with excitement. Many travelers had camped on this side of the city, too. Heli and Mary's walking pace was slower than in previous days, but Mary shook off her tiredness as excitement of seeing Elizabeth grew. Heli was deep in thought as they neared the small town. "How am I going to do this?" he wondered. "Zechariah will be in Jerusalem preparing for Passover. If Elizabeth is with child, should I be seen going into their house compound? If she is not ... well, the same question applies."

It was late morning as they approached the gate of Elizabeth and Zechariah's house. Carmen, Elizabeth's long-time servant girl, happened to open the gate at that very moment and recognized Heli. She immediately put down her market basket and went back inside, leaving the gate open. Heli and Mary could see a few women seated on the courtyard benches, most with their backs to them. Those seated were talking excitedly to someone sitting opposite of them. Carmen approached that person and bent to say something. Mary realized the "someone" was Elizabeth when she moved to peek between two heads. The obviously pregnant woman let out a joyous, "OH!" as she saw Heli and Mary. She placed her hand behind her back to help lift up her body from the bench and suddenly all heads turned toward the gate.

With Elizabeth

"Come, come in! Greetings! The Lord be with you, my dear cousins," Elizabeth said to Heli and Mary as she walked toward the gate.

Her eyes widened, "Is this my beautiful Mary? Oh, you have grown so much in four years!" Her eyes looked beyond them, "Is Johanna with you? Did the family come?"

The proper Jewish return greeting escaped Mary and Heli and Elizabeth's questions went unanswered. All they could see was Elizabeth's very round belly. Mary fell weeping into Elizabeth's arms. "Oh, Elizabeth!"

The embrace quickly ended, as Elizabeth pushed Mary back, exclaiming, "Oh! The baby jumped when he heard your voice." She laughed, and then they embraced again. The neighbor ladies understood that family members had arrived and made various excuses to gracefully depart. Carmen started to leave as well, but Elizabeth instructed her, "Carmen, go upstairs and ask Zechariah to come down." Carmen quickly used the courtyard stairs to the second story where Zechariah was praying.

"Zechariah is here? Not in Jerusalem?" Heli asked, surprised. "I thought he would be there preparing for Passover."

Elizabeth smiled as she returned to her cushioned seat. "Well, he was excused this time because he is unable to offer the prayers that accompany the sacrifices and celebration."

Heli's follow-up question was not spoken because just as Zechariah joined them in the courtyard, the Holy Spirit suddenly filled Elizabeth as the Spirit revealed to her why Mary had come. She rose again from her seat, gave a glad cry and exclaimed to Mary, "God has blessed you above all women, and your child is blessed. Why am I so honored, that the mother of my Lord should visit me? When I heard your greeting, the baby in my womb jumped for joy. You are blessed because you believed that the Lord would do what he said."

Mary, the Lord's Servant

Heli stood in place astounded, but Mary was beyond relief at God's confirmation and prophecy through Elizabeth. She had believed the angel's words, but Elizabeth's words were vital to her heart. This is one she knows closely follows God who is giving her the same information that she had received from the angel. What a relief to Mary! She connected the angel's words and Elizabeth's greeting to prophecies she had heard over and over in the synagogue.

Mary closed her eyes, lifted her hands heavenward rejoicing in the Lord and said,

> Oh, how my soul praises the Lord. How my spirit rejoices in God my Savior!
> For he took notice of his lowly servant girl,
>   and from now on all generations will call me blessed.
> For the Mighty One is holy, and he has done great things for me.
> He shows mercy from generation to generation to all who fear him.
> His mighty arm has done tremendous things!
> He has scattered the proud and haughty ones.
> He has brought down princes from their thrones and exalted the humble.
> He has filled the hungry with good things and sent the rich away with empty hands.
> He has helped his servant Israel and remembered to be merciful.
> For he made this promise to our ancestors, to Abraham and his children forever.

Now everyone was in tears, including Heli. The Holy Spirit's presence was palpable. No doubt remained in Heli's mind and heart that Mary had been greatly honored by the God of Abraham, Isaac, and Jacob to be the mother of the Son of God! Elizabeth

With Elizabeth

had confirmed it. Filled with amazement, the four of them rejoiced together in the courtyard.

Heli realized suddenly that not one sound had come from Zechariah. He turned at first to Zechariah to ask, "How did you lose your voice, Zechariah?" Realizing he couldn't answer, Heli redirected his question toward Elizabeth. "And please fill us in on God's miracle you have experienced."

Elizabeth replied, "Let's go into the house and I will tell you what happened. Mary needs to sit down. I see tiredness on her face even as the glory of the Lord rests on her." She turned toward the house and began, "Carmen ... oh, thank you. I see you are already prepared to wash their feet."

Heli had intended to return immediately to Jerusalem after accompanying Mary to Elizabeth's, but he needed to know how all this had come about, to understand for himself as well as to relay the amazing miracle to Johanna.

Elizabeth instructed Carmen to bring water, fruit, and breads to their unexpected company. After Carmen brought water and left to begin preparing the food, Elizabeth told the story, glancing at Zechariah occasionally to make sure she was telling it exactly right.

"You know that Zechariah serves with the Abijah division of priests one week every six months at the Temple. Just over six months ago, as was the custom of the priests, he was chosen by lot to enter the sanctuary of the Lord and burn incense. While the incense was being burned, a great crowd stood outside, praying. While Zechariah was in the sanctuary, an angel of the Lord appeared to him, standing at the right side of the incense altar. Zechariah was shaken and overwhelmed with fear when he saw him. But the angel said, 'Don't be afraid, Zechariah! God has heard your prayer. Your wife, Elizabeth, will give you a son, and you are to name him John. You will have great joy and gladness, and many will rejoice at his birth, for he will be great in the eyes of the Lord. He must never touch wine or other alcoholic drink. He will be filled with the Holy

Mary, the Lord's Servant

Spirit, even before his birth. And he will turn many Israelites to the Lord their God. He will be a man with the spirit and power of Elijah. He will prepare the people for the coming of the Lord. He will turn the hearts of the fathers to their children, and he will cause those who are rebellious to accept the wisdom of the godly.'"

Elizabeth paused and again looked at Zechariah. He closed his eyes and nodded for her to continue.

"Zechariah said to the angel, 'How can I be sure this will happen? I'm an old man now, and my wife is also well along in years.'

"Then the angel said, 'I am Gabriel! I stand in the very presence of God. It was he who sent me to bring you this good news! But now, since you didn't believe what I said, you will be silent and unable to speak until the child is born. For my words will certainly be fulfilled at the proper time.'

"While this was happening in the Holy Place, the people were waiting for Zechariah to come out of the sanctuary, wondering why he was taking so long. When he finally did come out, he couldn't speak to them. Then they realized from his gestures and his silence that he must have seen a vision in the sanctuary. He finished his week of service at the Temple and came home, telling me by gestures and by writing on a tablet what had happened. We rejoiced together at God's promise and within the month, I was with child. Of course I was ecstatic, but frankly so amazed and uncertain of the reaction of my neighbors that I stayed inside for five months before my good neighbor basically forced her way into my house" — she glanced at Zechariah, "Thank you for insisting I talk with her, Zechariah — and I told her my story." She looked at Mary, "I will tell you more about that if I have time later."

Turning to Heli, she confessed, "That's why I didn't send a message to Johanna. Please convey to her that now I know I should have." She continued to both of them, "In this past month the neighbor ladies have been here almost every day to rejoice with me and to help in whatever way they can. But I am so delighted

With Elizabeth

that you are here, Mary. Can you stay for a while, please? I can see you need to rest. We will talk about the prophecies of the Messiah. Zechariah can help, even without a voice. We have learned to communicate pretty well, even if it is with gestures and writing a few words on a tablet." She turned to Heli, "I believe Mary was sent here for this purpose."

"Yes," Heli answered. "I agree. I told Mary she should return to Nazareth with me when I come to the Pentecost festival. For now, time is getting away. I need to get back to Jerusalem before Nahum and Caleb think I am completely lost. Mary can fill you in on all that has happened at our house."

Heli said his goodbyes to Zechariah and then to the two amazing women, leaving them in the care of the silent Zechariah. A lot of talking would happen in this house in the next two months, but not from Zechariah.

Heli had a lot to think about on his way back to Jerusalem, including whether he should tell the others about the miracle child expected by Elizabeth and Zechariah. Yes, definitely, yes. That would help in the future when Mary returned to Nazareth. But he should not mention what else transpired during the short time he was at the house in Ein Kerem. Was Mary with child yet? He didn't know for sure. Mary seemed to indicate so and Elizabeth's greeting certainly indicated that. But it just didn't seem quite right yet to announce that his daughter was going to be the mother of the Messiah. He was still puzzled about how all this would transpire. His own words to his fellow travelers returned to him: "God will reveal all that we need to know when we need to know it."

As Heli left, Elizabeth looked at Mary and suggested that she lie down for a rest, and Mary certainly did not resist. The bed was as luxurious as Mary remembered from her previous visit. She fell asleep easily, as though sleeping on a cloud. It was past mid-afternoon before she stirred, refreshed and definitely hungry. Elizabeth greeted her and informed Mary they had been invited to share the

Mary, the Lord's Servant

Passover meal with the neighbors because of their small household number, as instructed in the Law. They had an hour or so before needing to be there so they had a bit of time for visiting.

Elizabeth could hardly contain her excitement. "Please tell me how you knew to come to me. How is it you know that you will be our Lord's mother?" She had patiently waited while Mary rested and she could wait no longer.

Mary took a deep breath, closed her eyes and let out her breath with a sigh. She looked into the eyes of Elizabeth and Zechariah. They were joyously anticipating hearing of Mary's experience, so freeing after her father's warning to tell no one in Nazareth. Where to begin? Hunger faded away as Mary began, "I am pledged to be married, Elizabeth."

"Oh ..." Elizabeth hadn't known yet about this happy news. Wasn't it happy news? Mary looked concerned.

"We had our engagement announcement party four months ago." Mary continued. "Joseph, my betrothed, is a wonderful man. He does not know anything about this yet. I have no idea how he is going to react ..." Mary paused, and Elizabeth reached out and squeezed her hand reassuringly.

"Yahweh knows, Mary. Go on."

"I will tell you more about him sometime later. The day — six days ago, just two days before Papa and Caleb and the others were to leave to come to Passover — was an ordinary day." Mary shrugged. "Nothing special about it, really. Mama asked me to fill a small jar with water from the village spring, so I did. It was unusual that I didn't see anyone on the way back home and just before I turned the corner to the house, I was startled by an angel in the path. Oh, Zechariah, I think this angel might have been the same one who appeared to you in the Temple. His bright white clothing, the suddenness of his appearance was so frightening, yet he was gentle.

"He said, 'Greetings, favored woman! The Lord is with you.' My heart was pounding, and my mind had a hard time at first taking it all in. The angel continued, 'Don't be afraid, Mary, for you have found favor with God. You will conceive and give birth to a son, and you will name him Jesus. He will be very great and will be called the Son of the Most High. The Lord God will give him the throne of his ancestor David. And he will reign over Israel forever; his Kingdom will never end!'"

Tears welled up and spilled down Elizabeth's and Zechariah's faces as Mary spoke and Elizabeth whispered, "Yes, the Messiah!" They were both as overwhelmed with the angel's message as Mary had been.

"I asked the angel how this would happen since the angel was indicating this would begin now but Joseph and I will not come together as husband and wife until later this year. The angel replied, 'The Holy Spirit will come upon you, and the power of the Most High will overshadow you. So the baby to be born will be holy, and he will be called the Son of God.' I felt the presence of the Holy Spirit even then. It was such a holy moment. Then the angel said, 'What's more, your relative Elizabeth has become pregnant in her old age! People used to say she was barren, but she has conceived a son and is now in her sixth month. For nothing is impossible with God.' That's how I knew. I think God told me about you as a confirmation that what he had said to me truly would happen. I just replied, 'I am the Lord's servant. May everything you have said about me come true.'

"I was rather stunned, I think, as the angel left, and could hardly walk. When I got home I told Mama and she was as shocked as I was. We talked about it and then told Papa when he came home. He had to think and pray about this sudden news for a while, but he was the one to suggest that I come immediately to you, even though Mama and I had already talked about it. Papa didn't think we should tell anyone, not even Buppy, Nahum, Esther, or the children, about this until we had come here and confirmed that you are indeed with child."

Elizabeth let out a small chuckle as she patted her belly and the child inside her. "Yes, indeed, I am with child. And the angel's word to Zechariah said that our child will prepare the people for the Lord. Our sons will be connected in ministry, Mary. That is marvelous! How wonderful are the ways of Jehovah our God!"

Elizabeth and Mary were silent for several moments as they all took in the wonderful news that had been shared. Then hunger reminded them they would soon need to walk next door.

Elizabeth almost giggled. "We will have time to talk about this in the upcoming days and explore the Word of God that is in our hearts. For now we need to go eat and celebrate Passover."

After they returned home, Mary and Elizabeth talked about how wonderful God was to them to bind together the ministries of their two sons. How amazing that God's time had been revealed — now the Messiah and His messenger would be coming into the world. Everyone had been waiting so long for this good news! What would be their roles in the Messiah's future Kingdom? Already Zechariah's mind was racing to the many passages of Scripture that spoke of the Messiah. In the coming days, he would invite his closest friend, Aaron, also a Levitical priest, to share verbally many Scriptures. Their home would be filled with God's Word and praises to their God.

Heli returned to the campsite on the northern slopes of the Mount of Olives. The Passover meal had been prepared in accordance with the Law and family traditions passed down by previous generations. Heli was delighted to share the marvelous news of Zechariah and Elizabeth's miracle before the group retired for the night.

The following morning thousands of worshippers gathered on the Temple grounds and worshipped God together as had been ordained by God and recorded by Moses in the Law. That day everyone's attitude was one of praise, worship, and prayer. As the throng inched their way from the Temple complex, among the thousands of worshippers Heli heard his name being called. He searched the crowd for the one who had called his name and saw Joseph weaving his way toward him. Concern was etched on Joseph's face. "Mary's here? I heard she came with you. Where is she?"

Heli motioned for Joseph to follow him to a less crowded spot as the moving throng of people carried the others on toward the Eastern Gate, also known as the Golden Gate. They managed to find a bit of breathing space just beyond the Temple gate. Heli did not intend to give Joseph full information, just enough to relay his fears for Mary.

"Yes, Mary wanted to come to visit her mother's cousin Elizabeth in Ein Kerem and felt it was urgent to do so now. And since we were traveling this way, she quickly got ready and came with our group from Nazareth," Heli explained.

"Why?" asked Joseph. "Why did she have to come now? I don't understand."

"Joseph, an amazing miracle has happened. Elizabeth has been childless during their forty-five-year marriage, but she and her husband have always desired and prayed to have a child. Zechariah was lighting incense in the Temple six months ago when an angel appeared to him and told him his prayers had been answered. He had a hard time believing how that could be since his wife was beyond child-bearing age, so the angel — he identified himself as Gabriel! — told Zechariah he would not be able to speak until the baby is born. Elizabeth is now in her sixth month. Mary is with her and will help her for a short time before she returns to Nazareth."

Joseph nodded, taking in this God-inspired information, not entirely understanding why Mary knew to come now or why she needed to come at all, so as though reading Joseph's thoughts, Heli added, "Johanna could not come because she is caring for our two nephews along with our two younger sons. Mary already knows Elizabeth and with Zechariah not being able to speak, Mary can be of great help to her. I took her to Ein Kerem yesterday morning.

Mary, the Lord's Servant

Mary will have plenty of time to rest before she returns to Nazareth, perhaps not until after Pentecost."

Joseph raised his eyebrows at Heli's indication of Mary's long visit, away from home just a few months before their marriage ceremony. But Joseph also knew he could not take the time after Passover and the Feast of Unleavened Bread to make the walk to Ein Kerem, visit with Mary, and then return home. Too much work awaited him.

Heli put his hand on Joseph's shoulder. "I need to catch up with the Nazareth group, Joseph. Mary is in good hands. It is good to see you in this throng. May God give you a good night's rest." Heli quickly left before Joseph had time to ask any other questions. No doubt he would have more when they had returned to Nazareth, and Joseph had time to wonder why Mary hadn't mentioned the possibility of her journey in the days before he had left for Cana.

CHAPTER FOUR
MARY'S HOMECOMING

Mary retired to bed early with thoughts of the wonders that she had learned and the amazing words she had spoken by the power of the Spirit, wondering what would come to light in the days — even years — ahead. She wondered how she could be so weary and so exhilarated at the same time. The nap she had earlier in the day did not prevent her from drifting off to sleep as if on a cloud.

Both Elizabeth and Mary had thought of questions to ask each other by the time they met in the morning. But the questions were set aside as Passover was observed in the household even without a trip to Jerusalem. What a special day it was with heightened importance as they rejoiced for God's provision for their ancestors in bringing them out of bondage in Egypt. They also wondered if God would now do the same for the current-day nation of Israel in ridding them of the rule of the Romans through the coming Messiah.

That evening, at the close of Passover at sundown, Elizabeth instructed Carmen to light lamps and prepare a meal of celebration, then she turned again to Mary and said. "Tell me about Joseph."

Mary's eyes lit up as she spoke of his dedication to the Lord, his participation at the synagogue, his legendary skills in stone masonry and carpentry, and the fun of their engagement announcement celebration. Mary extolled all of his great qualities, obviously

Mary, the Lord's Servant

quite taken with her future husband. And then she stopped. "But what if he doesn't believe me about the angel? What if he turns his back on me? What if ... ?"

"Mary," Elizabeth gently interrupted. "God will not abandon you. Perhaps God chose you not only because you 'found favor' with Him and have all the right qualities to be 'the mother of my Lord' but also because Joseph will be a good step-father to the Son of God. God will work it all out. This is where trust in the Father's plan comes in. He knows you. He knows Joseph. I don't know what will happen, but I know God will take care of you and His Son."

"Oh, yes. I do trust Him," Mary affirmed. "I know I need to take only one step at a time. Right now I am here with you because I am supposed to be here. God wants me to be here to learn all I can from you," she grinned and glanced sideways at Zechariah, "and from Zechariah even though he doesn't have a voice. Please, Elizabeth, tell me more about why you hid yourself for five months without telling anyone about your miracle."

"You know that all our lives Zechariah and I have desired to have a child," Elizabeth began. "The ladies of the village didn't ostracize me, but I know I got left out of many things because I am ... was ... childless. Think about these women from our history: remember how Sarah, Abraham's wife, reacted when she heard the angel say that she would have a son? She was also well beyond the age of child bearing, and she laughed, but then wouldn't admit she had laughed. And Rachel could not have children for a long time until God enabled her to conceive her son Joseph. Hannah begged the Lord at the Tabernacle in Shiloh for a child and Eli thought she was drunk! But God heard her prayers and her child Samuel became a prophet greatly used of the Lord.

"I spent those five months remembering all these women who begged the Lord for a child and how He remarkably answered their prayers and allowed them to experience the wonders of becoming a mother; then He used their children for His purposes. I asked

Mary's Homecoming

Zechariah to share with me anything he could think of from our history of these instances. And I have prayed and wondered what our child will face and how he — can you believe it? We know our child is a boy! — how he will be used by God in His great Kingdom. I didn't know about your wonderful news and connection to all this, but it is totally amazing what God has already done and what He is bringing about." Elizabeth drew in her breath as her son gave her another good kick. "Well, he is going to be a strong and lively one!"

Mary laughed. She looked forward to feeling the kicks and jabs of the child within her belly. But she was still concerned about what would happen as she returned to Nazareth, to her family … . Would she be returning to Joseph, too?

The next seven weeks seemed to fly by. Day by day, Elizabeth's baby grew along with her belly. Mary and Elizabeth talked about their future and the future of their sons. About prophecies. Mary learned that the Messiah was to be born in Bethlehem. Bethlehem? How? Why did God choose her? She lived in Nazareth! How was the birth going to happen in Bethlehem? And then Aaron, Zechariah's friend, pointed out that Isaiah had prophesied, "The virgin will conceive a child! She will give birth to a son and will call him Immanuel (which means 'God is with us')."

Mary's eyes had widened and she drew in a breath when she was reminded of that. "Amazing!" she marveled. "That's me! God told Isaiah about ME seven hundred years ago!" She once again was so humbled to be part of God's long-time planning for the redemption of Israel. The Messiah would be called "Wonderful Counselor, Mighty God, Everlasting Father, Prince of Peace." And Isaiah had said that "his government and its peace will never end," and "he will rule … from the throne of his ancestor David for all eternity." God gave Isaiah this prophecy seven hundred years before the angel had told Mary that her son, who is the Son of the

Most High, would be given "the throne of his ancestor David. And he will reign over Israel forever; his Kingdom will never end."

Mary was overwhelmed with all these prophecies and with the realization that she was involved in God's grand plan for all of history and into eternity. Mary and Elizabeth, along with silent Zechariah, prayed, cried, rested, and passed each day in blessed hope for the future. Mary also enjoyed getting to know Elizabeth's neighbors, who were so excited about Elizabeth's coming baby. Mary joined in when they gathered to sew baby clothes and to do their own embroidery work.

But the Feast of Pentecost was rapidly approaching and Mary was to return to Nazareth with her father at that time. Elizabeth was now almost eight months into her pregnancy, and she wanted Mary to stay longer. The time with Mary had been so amazingly fruitful for them both. Then one day in late spring, the day after the Pentecost celebration concluded, came a knock on the door.

Carmen ushered Heli and Caleb into the main room of the house. Mary gave a squeal of delight mixed with dismay. As she ran to greet her father and brother, Mary especially noticed the look of curiosity, perhaps even dread, on Caleb's face. She was to learn later that Heli had told Caleb the entire story as they walked to Jerusalem for the Pentecost celebration. He had learned during their Passover trip along with the others that his elderly cousin was to have a miracle child. During this trip he was shocked, incredulous that his sister — HIS SISTER! — was to be the mother of the Messiah. Mary's small frame already showed a small baby bump but that might be attributed to the healthy and abundant food that had been in front of her for the past almost two months. Mary glowed with the excitement of being with child, armed with the knowledge that she was indeed "the Lord's servant." God had equipped her in these weeks with the absolute assurance of His plan for her.

"Oh, Papa, it seems so long and yet so short since I have seen you," Mary said as she gave him a hug. She turned to Caleb. "Greetings, my brother. It must be that Papa has filled you in on our amazing news." Caleb only nodded, still adjusting to the new circumstances.

Heli immediately saw that Mary had gained maturity and poise in this short time and that Elizabeth already looked like she was ready to give birth to her child. She arose much more slowly than she had just seven weeks earlier. Healthy, but indeed great with child. Zechariah still could not talk but his embrace warmly greeted his wife's cousin by marriage. He was smiling too. "So," thought Heli, "he has not been completely worn down by weeks of incessant chatter of the two women."

Elizabeth indicated where they should sit to allow Carmen to wash their road-dusty feet and then offered them cool water and refreshments after their journey. Heli could almost tell what was in the air before Elizabeth began, "Please allow Mary to stay longer. I need her. I really need her to stay."

"But I am not going to be back in Jerusalem for quite some time. Mary needs to get home ... to find out ... what may happen." Heli almost added "... whether Joseph still wants her as his wife," but he didn't say it.

Elizabeth furrowed her brow. "You mean you still haven't told Joseph? He knows nothing of this?"

"No, he knows about your miracle child, but I have not told him about Mary's encounter with the angel. I think that is Mary's place. We will arrange a meeting with him at our house when we get back." Heli waited for a response from Mary or Elizabeth, but both were silent. He looked directly at Mary and said gently, "He is expecting you to come home with me ... now."

Elizabeth adjusted her sitting position to give herself time to think, then she said, "I do think Mary should stay another week or two, maybe three, or longer. I would prefer that she would help me

Mary, the Lord's Servant

until after the baby is here. If Zechariah can arrange for safe travel for Mary sometime in another month or so, can she stay until then?"

Heli had not anticipated this request when he brought Caleb along. He wanted to respond with a definite no, but something in Elizabeth's request and Mary's expectant face prompted him to ask, "Is that possible?" He looked at Zechariah, who quickly nodded. The conversation continued for a brief time with each one, except Zechariah, contributing their thoughts. Finally Heli concluded, "Let me think and pray about this and let you know in the morning."

The evening passed with some strain in the conversation, but Heli observed the ease with which Mary ministered to Elizabeth and the connection they had. Mary reviewed with Heli and Caleb the prophecies that had been discussed in the preceding weeks, but didn't mention an important one — that the Messiah would be born in Bethlehem. That would be up to God to accomplish!

In the morning, Heli agreed that Mary could stay if Zechariah could find a way home for Mary under one condition — Caleb would stay and accompany Mary home. Heli had already spoken with Caleb, promising him that Heli would either personally take care of or arrange for someone else to take care of Caleb's shepherding responsibilities since the sheep shearing was completed and the wheat harvest had not yet begun. Mary and Caleb would need to be home in three weeks so Caleb could help in his father's field. Zechariah nodded in agreement.

"Three weeks?" Elizabeth hesitated. That would mean Mary would not likely be there for the birth of her son, unless the little one made an early appearance. But it was probably a good compromise with Heli. That would give her more time to enjoy Mary and time to get to know Caleb better.

The decision was that Zechariah would take Caleb with him when he went to Aaron's house first thing that morning to inquire if Aaron was aware of any travelers going north in upcoming weeks. If Aaron, also a priest, did not know of anyone planning to travel,

Zechariah and Caleb would go with Heli to Jerusalem and have Caleb be his voice as he inquired about travelers going north in two or three weeks. Elizabeth so very much wanted Mary to stay at least a bit longer, and Zechariah would do anything for his wife.

Aaron had just returned from Jerusalem but was unaware of the possibility of later travel groups to the north. So the three men walked to Jerusalem so Heli could connect with a group heading north from the Pentecost celebration and Zechariah could locate a future group traveling north. Before Heli left their company, they stopped at a vendor of palm dates, intending just to purchase dates for travel food for Heli and a supply for Caleb and Zechariah to take back to Ein Kerem.

A casual statement between Heli and Caleb regarding traveling north soon prompted the merchant to remark that he was planning to travel to Damascus in three weeks. The men looked at each other with questions in their eyes—*Is this God's plan?* They wondered. *Does He work through food vendors?* After asking the merchant some questions, they felt it would be a good fit for Mary and Caleb to join this caravan of Israeli merchants. The merchant's wife and young daughter were to travel with him as well as several other merchants. Three weeks was longer than Heli wished, but he knew it would delight Mary and Elizabeth. Caleb was willing to remain with Zechariah and Elizabeth for that period of time, hoping to make contact with shepherds in the hill country surrounding Ein Kerem to observe their practices of shepherding. Arrangements for a meeting point were made with the merchant.

So the men all left Jerusalem — Heli heading to Nazareth and Caleb and Zechariah returning to Ein Kerem. Mary and Elizabeth were happy when they returned bringing good news and good dates! For three more weeks, they reviewed their discussions of the previous seven weeks. Elizabeth insisted on providing a sturdy pair of sandals for Mary. Elizabeth also had a new dress with more fullness made for Mary to accommodate her figure as it grew. Caleb

Mary, the Lord's Servant

made contacts with the shepherds of the hill country and spent a few days with them, comparing their shepherding practices with what he had already learned from his uncle. He returned to Ein Kerem more determined than ever to begin his own flock.

In three weeks less one day after Heli had left, Elizabeth, Zechariah, and Carmen more than adequately equipped Mary and Caleb for the trip back to Nazareth. With tears, sighs, and prayers, Mary parted ways with her dear cousin, now only days from delivering the miracle child promised by Gabriel. Caleb urged Mary to hurry her final goodbyes so they could arrive in Jerusalem at an inn for their overnight stay before leaving with the merchants' caravan in the early morning. Brother and sister began their walk to Jerusalem, this time with Mary's blanket folded around her new dress and her Sabbath dress along with her nearly worn out sandals and fashioned to carry on her back. Caleb carried the bag of food plus his own change of clothes.

The bed at the inn was certainly not as comfortable as the bed at Elizabeth's house, and Mary slept fitfully through the warm summer night, knowing that now she was on her way to face Joseph. One of David's songs that Elizabeth had quoted to her floated through her mind:

> Those who live in the shelter of the Most High
> > will find rest in the shadow of the Almighty.
> This I declare about the Lord: He alone is my refuge, my
> > place of safety;
> he is my God, and I trust in him … .
> For he will order his angels to protect you wherever
> > you go.
> They will hold you up with their hands.

At break of day, Caleb and Mary met the merchant Hirah and Miriam, his wife, and their ten-year-old daughter, Keren, among the camels outside of Jerusalem in the Kidron Valley. They had been assigned to walk with Hirah's family in the middle of the caravan. And so the trip home began. The atmosphere of traveling with merchants among camels was strikingly different than traveling with pilgrims toward a festival in Jerusalem. Mary did discover quickly that she must watch where she put her feet since they were following several camels and donkeys in the caravan.

Miriam was excited to be going on this trip since her family lived in Damascus, so during the first day she talked mostly about them and her joy at being allowed to return there. Little Keren was less animated in the conversation but did join in. Thankfully, after only a few hours, Miriam offered to place Mary's travel pack on her donkey's load, and Mary was relieved to walk without the extra weight and warmth.

It was Keren who asked, toward the end of the first day, "Are you going to have a baby?" It was windy, and evidently Mary's draped dress (she had opted for not wearing the usual belt) had blown against her body and revealed her almost-three-month baby bump.

Mary glanced at Caleb as he turned around at the question. *How do I answer that?* Mary thought. *Truthfully,* she decided. "Yes, I am. My brother is traveling with me since my ... Joseph is busy in Nazareth. He is a builder; he works both as a stone mason and a carpenter." Mary had already had a brief conversation about being in Ein Kerem with her cousin who was about to have a child. Fortunately, the child's curiosity was satisfied and her attention diverted to talking about their fine house in upper Jerusalem: the mosaic floors, the frescos on the walls, and her bedroom on the second floor that had a view of the Temple. Soon Mary found a break in the child's descriptions and walked a few steps ahead to walk with Caleb for a while and retreated into speculative thought about what awaited her at the end of this journey.

Mary, the Lord's Servant

The rest of the trip with the caravan went as smoothly as hoped although Mary missed the conversations previously shared with the group that had walked south over ten weeks earlier. Almost three months had passed. Mary was anxious to see her mother and younger brothers, but what would happen when she told Joseph the events of the past three months? Would he fully accept the mantle of earthly father to Jesus, the child she now carried, or would he turn his back on her?

On the third day, just past Scythopolis, the north-south road that continued to Damascus met the east-west road through the Jezreel Valley. Merchants traveled both of these roads, but Hirah and his family continued north. Caleb and Mary had already met and talked with just a few merchants who were heading west. Mount Precipice was already in view and only hours away. Mary retrieved her blanket, dresses, and sandals from Miriam's donkey's back and thanked Miriam for her kindness.

The sun had less than two hours before it touched the horizon when Caleb and Mary turned north onto the road, certainly a less-traveled path, up Mount Precipice toward Nazareth. This was familiar ground, and they would be home in a few minutes. Caleb reached for Mary's hand and helped her up the slope of the path. Amos and Simon must have been watching for them because they spotted their siblings as soon as they reached the top of the ridge and started shouting, "Mary's home!" and "Here comes Caleb!" *So much for quietly returning home*, Mary thought. Mary took the load from her back and held it in her arms in front of her to conceal her slightly protruding belly.

A few women called greetings from their yards or came out from their houses. "Welcome home, Mary." By now everyone knew she had been gone to stay with her cousin, whom God had favored in her late years with the miracle of a coming baby. Mary smiled and returned their greetings.

Mary's Homecoming

Hannah came running from her house. "Mary!" she called as she rushed in for a hug. A few others also began to gather around and walk with her toward her home. "Mary, I am so anxious to talk with you, but I know you are tired. Please, let's get together tomorrow." Mary nodded, agreeing to talk with Hannah after she had time to rest.

Mary was only a few yards from the family compound entrance when her younger brothers ran up to her. "Let me take your blanket," called Amos, trying to be helpful.

"No, I will," argued Simon, as he jerked the load from Mary's hands.

"Children!" Johanna reprimanded the boys as she too ran up behind them. But at that moment—that uh-oh moment—Hannah saw what Mary had been hiding.

"Mary ... ? Are you ... ?" The words were hardly out of Hannah's mouth when Joseph rounded the corner and realized what the question was all about.

"Mary?" Mary turned to face Joseph. "Wha ... ?" For an agonizing moment the scene was frozen in time.

"It's not what you think, Joseph," Mary began. "Please let me explain." But Joseph was already walking away. "Joseph?"

The handful of neighbors standing there who had previously smiled at her return stood in silence, shock and scorn on their faces—except Hannah. She found her voice and it was dripping with disgust. "Goodbye, Mary." She turned and followed Joseph.

It was worse than she had imagined. Johanna immediately put her arm around her daughter and led her home. Caleb, not knowing how to handle the scorn of the neighbors, quickly walked ahead, headed for his bed at Abigail's house. Mary knew that before everyone went to sleep that night, the entire village would know that she was with child.

Mary, the Lord's Servant

Her heart ached. Elizabeth had said to be strong, that God would go before her, that He would provide for her, that He would make her path straight. That wasn't happening.

Johanna and Mary entered their home and sat down. Amos and Simon didn't quite understand what had caused the sudden uproar and change in atmosphere. "What happened?" Amos asked. Johanna was in no mood to explain things to the boys just then.

"I will tell you later, boys. Thank you for bringing Mary's things into the house. Please bring Mary some water from the jar." She silently held Mary's hand and waited for Mary to say something. The boys returned with a cup of water. "Thanks. Now please go outside and play."

"I'm glad to have you home, Mary." Her words were thick with concern, but she didn't know what else to add. They sat in silence for a few more minutes. "Your Papa won't be home until dark. He began the harvest yesterday without Caleb. He will be glad to have Caleb's help tomorrow. I am anxious to hear all you have to tell me about Elizabeth and the past three months but right now you need rest. Would you eat some bread and go to bed right now?"

Tears fell from Mary's eyes, and as Johanna embraced her, Mary's body shook with deep sobs. "Oh, Mama, it is worse than I thought it would be. What will Joseph do? Elizabeth told me to be strong, that it would all work out according to God's plan, but ... oh ... " And the tears started anew.

Again Johanna had no words. Her heart broke for her daughter. Her tears overflowed her eyes. The only thing she could think of to say was, "Mary, pray. Remember what the angel said. Hold to that. And pray."

Abigail and Esther came cautiously to welcome Mary, having already heard the reports of her arrival. Abigail held her arms out to Mary, accepting her granddaughter's plight, not yet knowing the circumstances. Mary silently surrendered to the brief embrace. Johanna saw that Esther was uncertain what to do, so Johanna

Mary's Homecoming

stated, "Mary is quite tired from her journey. We will explain everything to all the family soon, but for now she needs to rest." Abigail and Esther both nodded, quietly leaving Johanna and Mary alone.

Mary ate a few bites of bread, and sat there, almost paralyzed with heartbreak over not being able to explain to Joseph that her baby was wondrous news, not a betrayal or a calamity. She knew that according to the Law, her fate was up to Joseph since she was betrothed to him. He could break their engagement for her perceived unfaithfulness or even have her stoned. Her mind flashed to the report of the young girl from Cana who was stoned just months ago when she was found to be with child before she was married. Mary agreed with her mother — she needed to pray. And to go to bed to rest. She was just about to get up when Heli burst through the door. She jumped up and ran to him. "Papa!" His face revealed he knew what had happened, how Mary had been greeted then met with distain as she arrived home. He also knew Mary's fate was in Joseph's hands — no, in God's hands.

Heli hugged his daughter, but not tightly. When he released her, he looked into her red-rimmed eyes. "Mary," he said solemnly. "We must tell Joseph and maybe the villagers about the angel's visit. Perhaps it will save you from … . No, that won't be the outcome. You are carrying the Child of God. Whatever Joseph decides, God will care for you and His Son. Joseph is a good man, a righteous man. You need to go lie down, pray, and sleep, knowing you are in God's hands."

Mary nodded and obeyed her father. She didn't sleep for a while because it was not quite dark yet and the summer heat seemed oppressive. Heli had received the news of Mary's homecoming while he was still out in the field and had rushed home to be with her. The boys came in, and their "Where's Mary?" was met with "Shhhhh." They understood she was tired from her journey and needed sleep.

Mary, the Lord's Servant

Heli motioned for his wife and sons to follow him outside. In the yard he whispered to them, "Go to Buppy's house. I will get Esther and the boys and be there soon." With the family together, Heli explained the events of the past three months. They all marveled at God's blessing on their family, specifically on Mary, and prayed for God's guidance for the entire family.

CHAPTER FIVE

THE PARADE

Joseph wrestled with his thoughts – his mind and heart tumbled with disbelief, anger, pain, disappointment, confusion ... and love. Mary, his Mary, his future wife, had been unfaithful! *Why? How? Who? When?* She had not even looked at another man in his presence. She had been totally focused on him. *Had she been forced? What happened?* That was to be discussed and discovered later. Right now his mind should focus on what he should do.

He knew her fate was in his hands. The Law declared that he could have her stoned. No! He would not do that. Absolutely not! He could make an announcement of divorce; no, she must not be disgraced publicly, regardless of what had happened. He could just break the engagement quietly; they would no longer be engaged. Her parents would then decide her fate. They did not seem to be angry with her. When he talked with Heli at Passover three months ago, Heli had not indicated anything was wrong. When they went to Pentecost celebration just over three weeks ago, Joseph had expected Mary to come home with Heli then, but she had asked to stay, Heli said, to help Elizabeth a while longer. *Did something happened while she was with Elizabeth? Surely not. She was safe there.*

Joseph tried to pray but his prayers seemed ineffective, hollow. Finally he surrendered his emotions to the Lord, saying, "Lead me, Sovereign Lord. What shall I do?" Quickly, he decided on

Mary, the Lord's Servant

a quiet divorce — no public meeting, just a statement through the rabbi that he could no longer be Mary's future husband. That would end his involvement with the one he had thought for many months that his future would be wrapped around. Sadly, he settled on that decision.

Joseph walked the two minutes over to the rabbi's house and knocked on the doorframe. The rabbi's wife opened the door to him and gravely pointed him to the rabbi, who was sitting in a chair in the back of the house rubbing his forehead. Rabbi James looked up and said sadly, "I heard, but it is hard to believe. Mary has always been a wonderful girl."

Joseph cringed. He really didn't want to rehash all his jumbled thoughts.

"May I ask what you are going to do?" Rabbi James asked gently.

"Divorce," he barely whispered.

The rabbi nodded. "Would you like a meeting at the synagogue to publicly announce the divorce?"

Joseph shook his head. "No. Would you write a divorce paper and take it to her father tomorrow?"

"Yes. Joseph, I am so sorry … ." Rabbi James hesitated just long enough for Joseph to nod quickly and leave.

He walked briskly home, to his unfinished home he was working on, which he had planned to share with Mary. He wasn't hungry, he wasn't sleepy; he was greatly perplexed. He stretched out, face down on his bed, pleading, "Lord, what happened to Mary?"

Somewhere in the black of night — it seemed like hours — Joseph finally fell asleep. And as he slept, an angel of the Lord appeared to him in a dream. "Joseph, son of David," the angel said, "do not be afraid to take Mary as your wife. For the child within her was conceived by the Holy Spirit. And she will have a son, and you are to name him Jesus, for he will save his people from their sins."

The Parade

Joseph woke with a start. An angel! Mary was with child from the Holy Spirit! A son, to be named Jesus! Save his people from their sins? Amazing! Yes! Mary! His beloved Mary!

The sky only hinted of the pinks of morning. Joseph could hardly wait for the full morning light before he ran to the rabbi's house and knocked, then pounded on the door. He heard "Coming, coming" from inside before the door opened slightly and the night-clothed rabbi mumbled, "What? ... Joseph?"

"Don't write that paper of divorce, Rabbi James! Don't! I'm going to take Mary home to be my wife today. Make an announcement at tonight's Sabbath gathering that she is my wife!" Joseph nearly jumped with glee as the rabbi, surprised and pleased, agreed, hoping for an explanation after he was fully awake.

Knowing that Heli would be getting up early to get a start toward the wheat field, Joseph went directly to Heli and Johanna's house. He knocked gently as he heard the occupants stirring inside. Johanna cautiously opened the door. "Joseph!" she exclaimed. Heli turned around startled, eyes wide in the early morning light.

Joseph didn't wait to start his explanation for the unusual intrusion. "An angel spoke to me in a dream and told me Mary is with child because of the Holy Spirit! Did you already know this? Why didn't you tell me? The Messiah, Heli, the Messiah!" Joseph intended to speak softly but in his excitement, he wasn't as quiet as he thought. Mary, already awake, entered the room.

"Mary, did you hear me? An angel told me your child is the Messiah, conceived by the Holy Spirit! The angel also told me to take you home with me to be my wife. I want to do that today. Now."

A cry of joy, relief, delight — everything together — came from Mary as she glanced quickly at her parents and then ran to Joseph. They embraced in amazement at what the angel had told Joseph. His wife! Today she was to be his wife!

"An angel spoke to me, too, Joseph. Before I left for Jerusalem. I am so sorry I didn't come to tell you, but I can tell you all about

Mary, the Lord's Servant

it now." Mary's face lit up with their shared revelations from the angel.

"Mary, I have already told Rabbi James to make the marriage announcement at tonight's Sabbath meeting. Now that the sky is fully bright, I want to take you home with me so everyone in the village can witness it." He looked at Heli and Johanna, asking, "Will you escort us to my ... our home? Then tonight the announcement will be made." Both of Mary's parents nodded in agreement.

To Mary, Joseph said, "Everyone in the village knows you are with child. Now they will know that you are my wife. We can tell them about the angel visits, too."

Heli cautioned, "Some will believe you, some may not."

Joseph, still euphoric from the angel's announcement, said, "It's a risk we will need to take. God sending His Messiah at this point in Israel's history should be a great encouragement to everyone."

Heli looked at Johanna; they both nodded. The boys were awake and aware of the excitement in the air although they didn't quite understand it all. So Heli simply stated, "Mary is going home with Joseph as his wife. Right now. Please walk quietly behind us and then we will come right back for something to eat."

Heli stopped. "No wait. The rest of the family should join us. I'll go get Esther and the boys. Nahum and Matthias will be sorry they weren't here for this. Johanna, go get Caleb and see if Buppy can join us, too." With the family gathered, Joseph again shared the angel's message and the marriage parade that was about to happen. They all happily joined in.

Mary smiled at Joseph, took a deep breath, and placed her hand on arm he offered. This was her wedding parade — not what they had originally envisioned, but it was the one that God had orchestrated. "I am the Lord's servant" echoed in her mind. She was to be Joseph's wife! Today!

They walked slowly at first to get the neighbors' attention, smiling, talking with each other, and nodding at those who looked

The Parade

at them, confusion evident on their faces. Just a few hours ago, Joseph had been aghast at Mary being with child and now he was walking her purposefully to his house with her family, including her brothers and cousins, who weren't exactly walking solemnly. The meaning was not lost on the villagers. Joseph led them the long way around the village to his house so everyone would have a chance to witness this open statement: Joseph was taking Mary home to be his wife. Yes, the meaning was not lost, obvious to everyone, including Hannah, who stared wide-eyed. Joseph was taking responsibility for Mary and her child.

As they walked, Joseph confided in Mary, "The house isn't as finished as I had intended for it to be before you came to live with me. In fact this morning I ran out of the house before making proper arrangements for you. But we will work on that today. Is that all right?"

"Yes. That will be fine. I'm so glad you received an angel's message, too."

The "parade" ended as Mary and Joseph walked under the slanted roof that sheltered his carpentry shop and entered the house; then the family members walked the short way back to their compound, smiling and acknowledging their neighbors with a nod. No doubt tonight's synagogue meeting would be full!

Joseph watched as Mary glanced around. Yes, the room needed a woman's touch, but she would be so glad to accomplish that. A small table and single chair, the one she was currently sitting on, were along one wall, and a wooden shelf was perched high above the table upon which sat a few cooking instruments. A few baskets hung on pegs on other walls, holding a few other essentials. A small hearth, now empty, of course, was built into one wall for cooking and warmth on cold winter days. Joseph suddenly saw the inadequacies of his humble abode and quickly stated, "Mary, tell me what you would like for me to do, and we will make it a perfect home for us." He glanced at the small bed in the corner, adding,

Mary, the Lord's Servant

"You will sleep there, and I will make another bed for myself. I think that we should not come together as husband and wife until after the baby is born."

Mary nodded. He was being so protective of her and the child.

"Oh, and I will make a baby's bed," he excitedly added.

Mary touched her stomach and smiled. "Joseph, can we put aside all those decisions for now? I have so much to tell you about how all of this came about and about my visit to Elizabeth. You need to know this now that you have accepted the responsibility of caring for me and for the child that I carry — the Messiah, Joseph! I am still so amazed at all that has happened."

Joseph readily agreed and pulled a small bench from his workshop. First, he offered a bit of food he had. With the doors open to allow the summer breeze through, Mary slowly and thoroughly replayed the events of the previous three months to Joseph. Occasionally, Joseph rose from his seat and paced as he listened, smiling. Well, there wasn't much room for pacing, but he walked a few steps around the room, excited to hear of Mary's recent experiences. They rejoiced often in amazement of God's plan and that He had chosen them — the two of them — to be parents to and raise the Messiah, the Son of God. How was he going to be different from other children? What challenges would they face in his upbringing?

Joseph listened carefully to Mary, silent except for quietly saying, "I wish I had known, Mary." When he repeated it again as she finished, he added, "But this was all in God's plan. And now the whole village will know your reputation is not ruined, that God chose you and has honored you!"

"Will they believe us, Joseph?" asked Mary, remembering how they had instantly judged her the evening before. Even Joseph had instantly rejected her at that time. It had taken an angel to inform him of the truth.

The Parade

"I think they deserve to be told. Whether or not they accept it depends on them. When Rabbi James allows me to speak, I first will announce that you are now my wife," Joseph paused to take his new wife's hand, to look deep into her eyes, and smile, "then your father can explain your meeting with the angel, and that is how you knew to go to Elizabeth. That is a solid fact even if they haven't met Elizabeth and can't see her now. Your father may have you talk, but I don't know if he will be allowed to do so since this is a Sabbath meeting, not a town meeting. After tonight, we will simply go forward in building our lives together and preparing for the birth of your son ... our son."

In the late afternoon, there was a light knock on the door, and Johanna called, "Mary, you will want your Sabbath dress. And here is your blanket. We can bring the other things you have made later." She hesitated but was quickly and warmly greeted by the "newlyweds." Then Johanna continued, "Would both of you come to our house for the evening meal before we go to the synagogue?"

Mary looked at Joseph. "Yes, of course," he answered. "We have been reviewing recent events and rejoicing all day, hardly stopping to eat, but I am sure Mary is quite hungry. I don't have much food in the house. I often trade my work for a meal, but we will get other plans put into place now."

Johanna turned and went toward the door. "Come as soon as you can be ready. That will give us adequate time to discuss what we think will happen this evening."

"Thank you, Mama. That would be good." And Mary did realize she was quite hungry.

Joseph closed the door to the shop and lit a lamp for Mary. "You change in here while I wash out back. I will be back in a few minutes." He took a garment from a peg in the wall above the bed as he left.

"I have a considerate husband," grinned Mary to herself, and the "I have a husband" thought was still new to her. But she was concerned. Going to her parents' house for the evening meal didn't concern her, even though it meant walking past curious eyes, but going to the synagogue did.

Joseph returned wearing his Sabbath cloak and headdress. He had changed outside after washing because no one could see into his backyard. *Something I need to get used to*, thought Mary. *Many things I need to get used to.*

As they ate, Heli and Joseph agreed that Joseph and Mary would arrive at the synagogue just before the meeting began. Rabbi James would announce, "Joseph has taken Mary as his wife," and then Joseph would tell of his dream, simply, plainly. Then Heli would explain why Mary had suddenly gone to visit Elizabeth, including the angel's announcement to her. Those who heard would decide on their own how they would react.

It happened almost as they had expected. Sudden silence in the crowd as Mary and Joseph entered together, then whispers among the women and stares from the seated men. Mary stepped to the women's area at the side of the synagogue to stand by her mother. Joseph took a seat next to Heli. Rabbi James cleared his throat and began with a Sabbath prayer.

When the rabbi said, "Joseph has taken Mary as his wife," there were a few light nods as if saying, "That's what I saw this morning," and a few almost-smiles. Mary heard Hannah let out a sigh with "humph." Mary hoped she could restore their close friendship later. Then Rabbi James asked the new bridegroom to say a few words.

Joseph prefaced the telling of his dream and the angel's message with these words: "All of you helped Mary and me celebrate the announcement of our betrothal only seven months ago. We all rejoiced together, and we have been preparing for our wedding. Then Mary suddenly left and has been gone almost three months to visit her cousin Elizabeth. All of you have heard about the miracle of Elizabeth's child. When Mary returned yesterday, it was easy to see that she too is with child. I went home heartbroken, praying

The Parade

for God to help me. Then last night in a dream, an angel spoke to me." He paused as a murmur spread. "The angel said, 'Joseph, son of David, do not be afraid to take Mary as your wife. For the child within her was conceived by the Holy Spirit. And she will have a son, and you are to name him Jesus, for he will save his people from their sins.'" Again Joseph paused, this time to let the angel's message sink into their hearts. "So today I did what the angel told me to do."

Rabbi James questioned, "An angel, Joseph? An angel spoke to you?"

"Yes," Joseph said quietly. "Please let Heli tell you more."

Heli rose to walk to the middle of the room. As he quickly told Mary's story, the murmur increased as some gasped in surprise, some in joy, some in disbelief. Mary began to silently weep.

Rabbi James spoke for all of them, "You mean that Mary's child is the Messiah? The Messiah!?" He was trying to wrap his heart and teachings around that statement.

"Yes!" Joseph emphatically said, so no one could misunderstand.

"It will take some time to understand this, Joseph," Rabbi James struggled to put his thoughts into words. "Is God sending the Messiah to a young couple in Nazareth? Our tiny village? Not Jerusalem? I always have known Mary as a devout worshipper of our Lord. You too have earned my respect since coming to live in Nazareth. I know you would not make up something like this. But this is difficult to accept. I do pray God will deliver us. We have prayed so often for the Messiah to come. We know the Lord will keep His promises. I'm not sure what this means. Let us think and pray about this as we go forward in the days ahead."

The Rabbi read from the scroll of Isaiah as he had previously prepared, made only a few soft statements, and the meeting ended with some of the villagers greeting Joseph and Mary, rejoicing with them, others glancing at them quickly as they left the synagogue. Hannah was one of those who left quickly. Mary and Joseph

Mary, the Lord's Servant

walked closely together toward their now-shared home and prayed together for God's strength and guidance in the days and months, even years, ahead.

Joseph's bed wasn't exactly comfortable until Mary added her extra blanket underneath her body. Then she slept soundly until the morning's light. Joseph was already up, trying not to make noise to allow Mary to sleep as long as she could. But she wanted to get up and fix a first breakfast for her new husband. Concern over the reaction of some of the villagers, even Rabbi James' words, hung in the air but was overcome by the confidence and trust they had in God's plan.

As the days passed, Mary and Joseph could easily pick out which villagers believed their telling of the angels' messages and those who did not. Of course there were many who didn't know what to believe.

Mary's thoughts went to Elizabeth — John had arrived by this time. What joy he would bring to Elizabeth and Zechariah! Surely by now Zechariah had regained his voice. Mary knew for sure he was rejoicing with Elizabeth in their son's birth.

As the weeks melted into a month, Joseph and Mary's life in the village was accepted or at least tolerated. Their home was their haven. Outside of those four walls, some looked at them as the couple who couldn't wait. Tongues wagged, people speculating as to what happened that Mary suddenly went away, or maybe something had happened while Mary was away, or perhaps Mary wasn't as "good" as she seemed to be. Or were their stories of the angels' visits true? But inside their home, Mary and Joseph talked about being charged with the raising of the Son of God. Was this child going to be different from birth? When would he become King of Israel, how and when would he take "the throne of his ancestor David," as the angel had said?

The extra room was finished except the roof, which would have to be waterproofed after the third pressing of the olives. The first

The Parade

press produced the extra virgin olive oil and one-tenth was set aside for the Temple. The second press could also be used for cooking, and the third press was for the oil lamps. The pulp that remained was then spread on the roof, which, after drying would prevent the rain from seeping in. The olive harvest would start in two months. Since it rarely rained in August and September, Mary and Joseph prepared their sleeping room for occupation.

As Mary's baby grew steadily in these weeks, Mary enjoyed his movements and kicks. The young couple continued to remind each other of prophecies about the Messiah in the Psalms and the Prophets. Even Rabbi James seemed to be centered on reading those prophecies on the Sabbath. He cautiously believed Joseph's and Mary's reports of the visits of the angels but didn't instruct or insist that the villagers believe as he did. It was as Heli had first predicted: some believed them, and some questioned their stories.

Hannah slowly thawed in her attitude and relationship with Mary and by late summer had resumed her friendship with Mary. She had even allowed Mary to more thoroughly detail the events of those three momentous months. The two spent many hours together as Mary happily prepared for the birth of her baby. They had used Johanna's loom to make another blanket for Mary from the wool they spun, as demonstrated by Abigail. They prepared the baby clothes, blankets, and other necessities. And since Mary needed to finish furnishing their house, they also made small lamps, dishes, and water jars at the town's kiln.

The olive harvest was to start in late September, with Joseph anticipating purchasing olive pulp from Yonatan for waterproofing his roof. Joseph knew that Yonatan had previously promised the first and second batches of pulp to another villager. In fact, Joseph was to repair a leaky roof before working on his own roof. Joseph was glad for the job, which he would tackle as soon as he finished waterproofing the huge stone jar at the synagogue that held about twenty gallons of water. The synagogue at Nazareth was small and

Mary, the Lord's Servant

had only one jar to hold the water for ritual cleansing. Every year it needed to be re-plastered with a mixture similar to that which was used between the stones in building homes. Otherwise the water would easily seep through the walls of the huge limestone water jar.

Once the water jar was plastered and the other villager's roof repaired, Joseph would begin on his own roof. Mary looked forward to having more room in their little home.

CHAPTER SIX

TRAVELING TO BETHLEHEM

In early autumn, the quiet of the early evening was abruptly disrupted by the pounding of many horses' hooves coming into the village. The noise of the soldiers quickly drew all available villagers, including Joseph and Mary. The arrival of the Roman soldiers caused hearts to fear and beat faster, but the people were relieved as soon as they learned the reason for the soldiers' sudden appearance — an official announcement. The centurion and his soldiers from Sepphoris had been sent by King Herod who had instructed them to proclaim in all the Galilee villages that the Roman emperor, Caesar Augustus, had decreed a census would be taken throughout the Roman Empire.

A census would mean paying more taxes. The instruction was that all men would return to their own ancestral towns to register for this census. This must be accomplished within three new moons.

Each Israelite man could trace his ancestry back to Abraham. Mary looked quickly at Joseph. He was a descendant of King David, the tribe of Judah. Joseph's ancestral town was Bethlehem! Upon returning to their house, Mary and Joseph discussed the prophecy that the Messiah was to be born in Bethlehem. They would have to travel to Bethlehem soon. Mary was already in her sixth month.

Mary, the Lord's Servant

But the olive harvest had just begun and must be completed; Joseph then needed to immediately spread the olive pulp on the roof and complete other urgent and promised projects.

Heli and Nahum called a family meeting and after discussing the situation, it was agreed that Heli, Johanna, and Caleb would travel to Bethlehem almost immediately. Nahum and Esther, along with Matthias, could arrange care for the sheep so they would travel with them. Joseph and Mary would be in charge of her brothers and nephews; all four boys promised to be easy to care for. Other villagers were from other tribes and some would register nearby, but all would go to the town of their tribal leaders. Not long after that day, Joseph heard from his father and his family that the timing was right so that they too would be going to Bethlehem as soon as they could.

Heli and Nahum and their wives and older sons returned in two weeks and reported that many people were on the road to Jerusalem and then, as in their case, on to Bethlehem. The inn at Bethlehem had not been full when the brothers and their wives and sons were there, but they had been invited to stay in private homes. The residents of Bethlehem knew that those coming to their small town to be registered were of the tribe of Judah and thus related to most of Bethlehem's residents. Many of their homes had a guest room, and they were willing to share with family members.

It was Joseph's full intention for Mary and him to begin their trip within one, no more than two, months. Mary needed to arrive in Bethlehem, rest and get settled in before the baby came. Circumstances kept delaying their travel. Finally with only two weeks before the allotted time to register ended, Mary and Joseph were ready to begin their journey.

Johanna reminded Mary of the Lord's protection for her and the child, even though Johanna was quite uneasy at the delay in their departure. Heli embraced Joseph with no words, yet concern was etched on his face.

Traveling to Bethlehem

Joseph had purchased Yonatan's second donkey and had made a small cart to pull with their supplies, which included Joseph's tools. Mary had packed the rest of the cart as lightly as possible but needed to take along supplies for the baby, a few clothes, dishes, and cookware, and travel food. They would need to stay a short time in Bethlehem after the baby's birth so Mary could recover. The cart could be pulled by Joseph as Mary rode the donkey or pulled by the donkey as Mary walked short distances. Mary dreaded the days of travel. *How many will it take?* she wondered. Yet, anticipating the child's arrival, Mary and Joseph left Nazareth, not knowing for sure how long they would be gone.

As soon as they reached the Jezreel Valley, they encountered men, couples, even complete families on the road. Those of the tribe of Ephraim were headed to Shiloh; one couple of the tribe of Gad would be crossing the Jordan River just below the Jabbok River to register in Jazer; one man they talked to was going the farthest — to the area of the tribe of Simeon to register in Beersheba. At first they talked to no one headed to Bethlehem, but most travelers were moving faster than they were, many expressing concern for Mary in her condition. Occasionally they were traveling almost alone, praying for God's protection, until others caught up with them and traveled along with them until the others tired of Mary and Joseph's slow pace. Then Mary and Joseph were alone again. But they never felt abandoned by God. They knew He went with them.

Mary's thoughts returned to her trip on this road when she had come back to Nazareth only six months earlier and the reason she had traveled to Ein Kerem. "I must go to Elizabeth's house while we are close," she said to herself. "I wish we could have come earlier so we could have visited before the baby's arrival, but perhaps we can travel to Ein Kerem after he arrives. John is about six months old now. Oh, I want to meet him and to visit again with Elizabeth and Zechariah. And Joseph! They must meet Joseph and

Mary, the Lord's Servant

he must meet them." She passed time by replaying in her mind her previous visit to Ein Kerem and anticipated visiting again.

Each night they rested in the company of others. Each day repeated the first day's scenario. Sometimes traveling with others, sometimes alone but never feeling vulnerable. Instead of taking three days to reach Jerusalem, it took four and one-half days.

The sun was at its peak overhead and once again Mary thrilled at the sight of Jerusalem from the top of the Mount of Olives. Relief beyond expectation flooded both of them as they viewed the Temple, the great walls and gates of the city. Joseph suggested they find a real bed to sleep in rather than traveling on to Bethlehem that night. He knew the window of time for registering was closing, but it seemed many others had delayed until the last moment as well. One more day wouldn't make a difference.

Mary agreed, and they started down the steep slope on the western side of the Mount of Olives toward the Kidron Valley, then up into the city. Mary was riding on the donkey while Joseph pulled the cart. She was looking forward to seeing the city again. But just as they were about to start up toward the city gates, Mary felt the baby kick hard and her abdomen tightened in pressure, accompanied by a painful cramp.

"Joseph!" Mary cried out. Joseph quickly turned around to see Mary's hand on her abdomen and her face contorted in pain. "I think the baby is on his way soon, maybe today! Can we go on to Bethlehem instead of staying tonight in Jerusalem?"

Joseph was startled and anxious. "We can do that. Let's rest for just a short time and get some fresh food. We still have time to reach Bethlehem today. It is only five miles beyond Jerusalem."

Joseph was obviously hungry, but Mary was not. She was tired. Joseph found the food vendors along the outside west wall of the Temple complex and ate quickly as he watched Mary, seeing her occasionally wrinkle her brow. Joseph had helped her dismount from the donkey and sat her down on a chair the vendor offered.

Traveling to Bethlehem

He purchased some palm dates, Mary's favorite she had said. He would eat some now and save some for Mary when she wanted to eat. Joseph found other vendors nearby selling an adequate variety of foods, and he purchased a small amount for eating now and later.

Joseph was just about to suggest they begin to travel again when the noise of the crowd suddenly swelled, and the sharp sound of horses' hooves on the flat pavement stones grew louder and louder. People began shouting to get out of the way and shoved their way down the street. Joseph grabbed the donkey's rope and pulled their cart to an available spot on the opposite side of the street from Mary but didn't have time to come back for her. A frightened Mary moved as quickly as she could behind the vendor's cart at his invitation as he grabbed the chair and secured it under his awning.

The Roman soldiers expected everyone to clear the street as they marched behind the two centurions leading the foot soldiers. They were impressively dressed, true, but no cheers for them came from the Jewish crowd. What seemed like a huge number of soldiers — were there 50 or more? — marched by, obviously headed toward their home base, the Antonia Fortress, which had been erected next to the northern wall of the Temple complex. In fact, it had been built tall enough so the Roman soldiers stationed there could keep constant watch on the events and people within the Temple grounds. The Jews were allowed to practice their religion, but the Romans kept vigilant watch on the crowds. Just in case.

Suddenly new voices shouted further down the street in the direction the soldiers were heading. A centurion's command brought the soldiers to a stop. A few were ordered forward quickly toward the commotion, but Mary and Joseph along with everyone else were held in place as the soldiers evidently quelled a protest against their presence and arrested those who had challenged their authority. It seemed like a very long time before the soldiers continued on their way and cleared the street. Mary and Joseph were

Mary, the Lord's Servant

reunited, thankful that neither had been hurt and that their belongings were spared damage.

"What was that shouting?" Mary asked.

"It must have been some rebels," Joseph replied, "perhaps members of the Zealot group that seem to think they can overthrow the Roman rule. Let's get moving again." He hadn't intended for it to take this long to make what he thought was a short stop and to get through the many people on the streets of Jerusalem. Now it was urgent that they leave the city promptly.

The road to Bethlehem went south out of Jerusalem following the ridge on the hills to minimize elevation changes, much less hilly than the road from Jericho up into Jerusalem. Mary again rode on the donkey as Joseph pulled the small cart. Joseph could tell Mary was deep in thought, and occasionally the wrinkled forehead gave way to a grimace. Joseph wanted to hurry but at times Mary needed to stop for a few minutes and take deep breaths although she didn't dismount. *Shouldn't we hurry as quickly as possible?* Joseph thought. The baby was ". . . on his way soon," Mary had said earlier. Other travelers passed them even when they weren't stopped.

The five miles should have taken only two hours at the most but Joseph noticed deepening blue of the eastern sky and the hues of orange of the sinking sun on the city gates and the houses of Bethlehem as they ascended the hill into the small village, even smaller than Nazareth. Joseph had been told to inquire at the inn for a room, and the innkeepers would know if private homes had openings for visitors in their guest rooms.

Finally the inn came into view, but Joseph could tell it bustled with swarms of people. He and Mary made their way through the crowd until he saw a woman he judged to be in charge. "We need a room for the night" — he had stuck his head through the open door, and she glanced his way. She was busy and at first didn't acknowledge his request. So he repeated, "Please — we need a room for the night."

Traveling to Bethlehem

Hardly looking his way and obviously frazzled at serving the already overcrowded room, the woman said, "We are full; we have no room."

"Do you know of *any* homes that would accommodate my wife and me for the night? My wife is about to give birth," Joseph pleaded.

His tone got the woman's attention, and her countenance softened. She came toward the door and looked at Mary slightly bent over on the donkey, obviously "great with child."

"Oh, I am so sorry. We are full, and I do not know of any other places that are available in Bethlehem," she said, her face showing concern for the situation. "But," she offered, "we may be able to find some room in our stable, although we have already sent two others to bed down there for the night." She turned and raised her voice, "Azor, here's another couple to be shown the stable."

A young boy, perhaps about nine years old, came into view, and his mother added, "Take a lantern with you. They will need light to find a place to rest for the night." Then to Joseph she said, "I am sorry. This is our only availability."

A quick glance at Mary confirmed to Joseph that she urgently needed a place to rest. While the woman was still directing her son, a man made his way through the crowded room and heard the end of the conversation. The man was the owner of the inn, and Joseph was to learn later the innkeeper's name was Micah and his wife was Ethlan. The boy came back into the room having retrieved a lamp that he carried with a handle, and stepped through the door, motioning for Joseph to follow him.

"Son," the innkeeper called from the doorway. Azor paused and turned around. "Take them to Nathan's stable. He told me this morning he isn't bringing his sheep in for a couple more days; it is empty except for his donkey." The man looked at Joseph and explained, "He told me that I could send someone there if I needed to, and you need to get your wife into a shelter. Use the fresh straw

Mary, the Lord's Servant

to make a bed. And light the firewood stacked at the mouth of the cave for light and warmth. May Jehovah's blessings go with you."

Joseph sighed and gave a heartfelt, "Thank you; may God's blessings be yours," as they followed the boy down a rocky and not-well-used path toward a stable cave. "Soon, Mary, soon you can rest."

Mary straightened a bit, smiled, and took a deeper breath. "Oh, that will be so good."

CHAPTER SEVEN

"WOULD YOU LIKE TO HOLD THE BABY?"

Their destination was a bit further than the inn's stable, but it was quiet, and they gratefully looked into the smaller cave. The boy held out his hand for the donkey's rope so Joseph could help Mary dismount from the donkey. He turned to Joseph and said, "Better make your bed on that side," indicating the opposite side of the cave. "You will get light and warmth from the fire, but not the smoke from the burning wood."

Joseph nodded and led Mary to an empty stall. He quickly spread a good amount of loose straw on the ground. After he helped her carefully sit, and then to lie down, she said, "Oh, that feels so good. Thank you, Joseph."

As they entered, Joseph had noticed the small pile of dried wood, stacked and ready to light. To the back of the cave was a lone donkey, already bedded down for a rest. Azor led Joseph's donkey beyond where Mary was resting and handed the rope to Joseph. Joseph asked him to bring a small pail of water to be warmed by the fire. The boy returned shortly and set the pail near the wood pile. He left the lantern with them so Joseph could light the wood, then he ran out. After Joseph coaxed the wood to light, he moved the cart close to Mary and pulled out a blanket to cover her. Joseph

Mary, the Lord's Servant

ate some of the food he had purchased in Jerusalem, but Mary ate only a few bites. A peace settled over both of them, knowing their lives would drastically change in the next few hours.

Although the only birth Mary had witnessed was watching a lamb being born, her mother had instructed her as to what to expect. Johanna had hoped to be at Mary's side to be of assistance to her, but when Mary had reminded her of the prophecy that the baby was to be born in Bethlehem, Johanna had given her as much information as she could.

Joseph had been sleeping only a short time when he heard Mary gently groan and call out, "The baby is coming now, Joseph; help me get ready." Joseph brought the lamp close, and did as Mary guided him. He spoke softly to reassure her as she experienced the pain of giving birth. Thus the Son of God, the Messiah, came into the world he had created, but this Light of the world entered in the near-darkness of a stable cave.

Joseph dipped the cleaning cloth into the bucket of water that had been warmed by the fire and quickly wiped baby Jesus clean as the newborn let out a healthy cry. Both Mary and Joseph laughed and cried as they quickly rubbed him with salt, wrapped him snugly in strips of cloth as Mary had been instructed by Johanna, then added a warm blanket around him.

Mary tenderly brought the new baby to her breast for his first feeding. *Amazing!* she thought as she kissed his face. Joseph thought his heart would burst with relief and happiness, wondering at the same time how this child was to fulfill his mission as the Messiah.

Mary placed the sleeping baby, snugly wrapped, in the manger near her head. Joseph rearranged the straw to make a more comfortable bed for them both, and Mary closed her eyes, glad to lie back down. Joseph went to put another log on the fire at the mouth of the cave and returned to lie down.

He was about to blow out the lantern when he heard people talking loudly near the cave's entrance. He could tell they were

"Would You Like to Hold the Baby?"

coming nearer; then a torch appeared and an excited voice declared, "Here they are!" All the newcomers were talking excitedly at the same time: "Is there a baby in here?" "Praise be to God on high!" "You were right, Nathan—the Messiah is in your stable." "'Glory to God,' as the angels said." "The manger. The angel said we would find him in a manger."

Joseph and Mary were jolted fully awake by the exuberant entrance into the stable cave by five men—no, two men and three judged to be early teens or pre-teens, all shepherds.

"Yes," Joseph answered. "I am Joseph; this is my wife, Mary." He reached for sleeping Jesus in the manger and carefully picked him up. "This is Jesus. You say an angel spoke to you? Please tell us about it."

Since it was Nathan's stable and he seemed to be the one in charge, the other shepherds allowed him to tell the amazing story. "I was on watch and the others were sleeping near our sheep just over that hill" — he pointed to the left of the cave entrance — "just less than an hour ago. As quickly as a snap of a finger, an angel in bright clothing stood just a few feet away from us, and we were all suddenly awake and I'll admit I, we ..." he gestured to indicate all of them, "we were terrified! The angel lit up the night. I am surprised the whole countryside didn't see it! We could feel God's presence surrounding us. 'Don't be afraid!' the angel said. 'I bring you good news that will bring great joy to all the people. The Savior — yes, the Messiah, the Lord — has been born today in Bethlehem, the city of David. And you will recognize him by this sign: You will find a baby wrapped snugly in strips of cloth, lying in a manger.'" Nathan briefly paused to relive the wonder of the angel's message.

Joseph looked lovingly and with amazement at the sleeping bundle he had picked up from the manger, and tears once again welled up in Mary's eyes. God again was confirming His word to them and spreading the news to others that Jesus was the Messiah, the Savior, Christ the Lord!

Mary, the Lord's Servant

"But then ... ." One of the other shepherds could hardly wait for Nathan to continue, so Nathan was prompted to go on with the story.

"We thought that one angel was bright, but suddenly, the angel was joined by a vast host of others, the armies of heaven, praising God and saying, 'Glory to God in the highest heaven, and peace on earth to those with whom God is pleased.' They seemed to fill the sky and their voices seemed to echo through the heavens. Did you see the bright sky and hear the angels praising God? It didn't frighten the flock, but it sure scared and amazed us! Then as suddenly as they had come, they were gone.

"It took several minutes for us to find our voices and to see in the dark again. We tried to be quiet so we wouldn't awaken and frighten the flock, but we did whisper to each other, 'Let's go to Bethlehem! Let's see this thing that has happened, which the Lord has told us about!' We all agreed to come immediately and not wait until morning. When we approached Bethlehem from the west, we could see the fire at the mouth of my stable cave and decided we must look here first. We are sorry to bother you in the middle of the night, but we just couldn't wait until morning. You already know he is the Messiah, right?"

"Oh, yes," Joseph answered. "Angels have spoken to us also. Would you like for me to tell you how angels have spoken to us?"

"Yes!" the shepherds responded, several in unison.

"Would you like to hold the baby?" Mary quietly asked from behind Joseph. She had remained lying down but was as excited as Joseph was at the shepherds' encounter with the angels.

Nathan's eyes widened. "May I?" he asked as he handed the torch to one of the others. To Joseph he urged, "Please tell us about the angels you heard." He carefully took Jesus from Joseph's extended arms and thought his heart would burst from the holiness of the moment. He was holding the Messiah!

"Would You Like to Hold the Baby?"

Joseph gave the shepherds a brief summary of how the angel's announcement was made to Mary, about her three-month visit to her cousin's house to witness that miracle, about her return to Nazareth and the angel's message to Joseph. The shepherds listened as they gazed into the beautiful face of the sleeping baby. Joseph's telling took only a few minutes, but the shepherds realized that they, common shepherds, had been included in the miraculous story of the coming of the Messiah. The prayers of the whole nation had been answered by the birth of this child. His life began in a stable. How would it move forward to his fulfilling the prophecies about him, especially those about "the throne of David"?

The baby stirred and made a slight cry, so Nathan handed him back to Joseph, who returned him to the manger and Mary's watchful eye.

Nathan motioned to the other shepherds to depart. His voice was quiet. "We will leave now, but we will talk with you in the days to come. You need rest. You can't stay here; this is no place for the Messiah. We will find better accommodations for you soon."

As soon as the group was outside the cave, their voices' volume increased, reflecting with wonder the astounding events they had just experienced. Their voices faded away as they went up the path toward Nathan's house, which was located above the cave. Joseph and Mary were to learn later that the shepherds had awakened several neighbors with their rejoicing before they returned to the flock waiting in the field.

Mary and Joseph were just grateful to get a few brief hours of sleep before once again the baby stirred and needed to be fed and cared for.

The sky slowly became light, and Joseph arose, trying not to awaken Mary, but before he left the cave, she spoke to him. "That was a more than an eventful night," she smiled as she spoke. "Almost overwhelming. But I guess we will have many more wonderful events in our lives as we raise this child. Jehovah is a wonderful God. He will help us every day, one day at a time."

"He certainly will," Joseph agreed. "We must pray and depend on Him daily. For now, I am going to inquire about accomplishing the task that brought us here. I will find out where to register for the Roman government and find where I can buy us some food. Will you be comfortable being here alone while I am gone?"

Mary chuckled. "I'm fine. But I'm not alone." She gazed at the baby in the manger and reached to pick him up. "Yes, we will be fine."

Joseph stood at the entrance of the cave. It faced northwest and Joseph could see Jerusalem in the distance, although partially obscured by trees and hills. What stood out most was the tall Temple of God reflecting the early morning light. The sight thrilled him. He and Mary now had the responsibility of raising the Son of God! They currently were sheltering in a stable, their future ahead was uncertain, but God definitely reassured them by providing many angelic events to announce the Messiah's coming! Joseph was at peace with the confidence that God knew what He was doing. Everything was going according to the Lord's plan.

Joseph followed the path back toward the inn, now with fewer people milling about. He stepped inside to ask the innkeeper where he was to register. Instead he found Ethlan, the innkeeper's wife, who recognized Joseph as the expectant father she had seen the night before. "Where do I go to register for … ?" Joseph began.

She interrupted him: "How's your wife?"

Joseph smiled widely. "She's fine. We have a son, and both of them are resting."

Ethlan stopped her work and straightened up. "YOUR baby? Is that what the shepherds were making all the fuss about in the middle of the night?"

Joseph didn't even have time to answer before one of the inn's guests said grumpily, "So you're the reason our sleep was rudely

"Would You Like to Hold the Baby?"

interrupted. It's bad enough to sleep in this overcrowded inn, but then we were awakened by those rowdy vagrants shouting out in the street. We thought they were drunk, but they were just shouting about another baby being born, as if that's news. They even mentioned angels! Couldn't they have waited until daylight to cause all this commotion about your baby?"

Joseph smiled inside and thought, "*God* didn't wait until daylight to announce this baby's arrival." But he knew better than to argue with a grumpy, sleepy traveler and redirected his attention to the innkeeper, who had entered the room, and quietly asked his first question, "Where do I go to register for the census?"

"The synagogue," the innkeeper answered as he pointed Joseph in the right direction. And then quietly he added, "Congratulations on the birth of your son."

Joseph made his way toward the synagogue, which as in any Jewish town served as the town hall, the hub of the community. Inside was the local tax collector, acting as Rome's agent for the census. He was seated at a table and was asking questions of a man Joseph had seen the previous night at the inn. Another man waited to be interviewed and registered. Joseph noted that the agent was making notes on a parchment and as he finished, the one being interviewed produced coins from his bag, and the agent quickly placed them in a container sitting beside him. The agent called the next man up, talking quietly to him only a few minutes, making notes, again finishing with depositing coins in the jar beside his chair.

At last he motioned for Joseph to come to the table. His questions were crisp and Joseph answered as briefly as possible. *What is your name?* Joseph, son of Jacob. *You are from the tribe of Judah?* Yes. *Where are you currently residing?* In Nazareth. *What is your occupation?* I am a builder, a stone mason and a carpenter.

The questioner looked up. "We need one of those around here," he stated.

Mary, the Lord's Servant

The questioning continued. *Are you married?* Yes. *Wife's name?* Mary. *Do you have children?* (His question made Joseph smile.) Yes, one son. *How old?* He was born last night.

The questioner quickly looked up and frowned. "Were you out in the streets last night, yelling about your son's birth? The commotion disrupted my sleep!"

Before Joseph could say he was not in the streets although "the commotion" had been about his step-son — well, that might be too hard to explain briefly — the tax collector announced, "Pay me three silver denarius ... no, four — the extra for disturbing my sleep last night."

Joseph paused. The others had not been charged that much, but he really had no choice. Joseph was grateful he had adequate Roman coins to pay this tax, probably most of it going directly into the agent's pocket. Although it nearly depleted his funds, he knew he had to hand over the money; then he left the synagogue. At least he knew now where the synagogue was for the Sabbath, which began that evening. He headed back toward the inn to inquire this time about buying food to take to Mary.

Only a few minutes after Joseph had left Mary, she heard a woman's voice at the cave entrance. "Greetings! May I come in?"

"Yes, welcome," Mary called quietly so as not to disturb the baby.

"Hello, Mary. I am Rachel, Nathan's wife. He and his fellow shepherds are the ones who intruded on you last night. They came up to the house and told us about the angels and their announcement and about you and Joseph being down here and the baby — oh, the baby!" Rachel exclaimed as she looked at the babe resting beside Mary. Then Rachel quickly added, "Did you get any sleep at all? Where's Joseph?"

"I rested well the rest of the night, waking only once more to care for the baby," Mary replied. "Joseph went to register." She instantly liked Rachel, responding to the concern and excitement in her voice.

"Would You Like to Hold the Baby?"

"Mary, you cannot stay here, but I'm not sure what to do. We have guests in our tiny guest room, but they are not planning to leave until tomorrow. They came from near Mount Carmel. But, please, we want you to stay with us. They want to come to meet you and the baby and rejoice with you also, but I want them to wait until later in the day until you have rested more. Here's some food for you and Joseph." She handed Mary some wrapped flatbread, fruit, and several other food items.

"Thank you so much, Rachel." Mary reached out and took the bundle. "Joseph was going to buy food after registering, but I just realized how hungry I am. I didn't eat much yesterday. And thank you for trying to find us a place to stay. We stayed warm last night with the fire and our thick blankets, but we certainly would love to accept your invitation to stay with you when you have room."

"I will do what I can. Oh, is it true? Of course, it is!" Rachel answered her own question. "How exciting that the Messiah has come! Nathan was overjoyed as he told us about the angel and then the whole sky full of angels that brought the good news to them. He had to go back out to the field, but he hopes to bring the sheep into the cave in a day or two. I will be back when we get this all figured out." Rachel left, determined to make a way for this newborn and his parents to be in a proper bed before nightfall.

Mary ate part of what Rachel had brought and then laid back again. She pulled the blankets over herself and Jesus as they snuggled warmly together. Yes, it would be so good to be in a proper house, but God had provided all they had needed to this moment.

Joseph purchased only a little bit of food from the inn since he intended to then go to inquire about town to find a better place for his wife and newborn. He returned to Mary, finding her and Jesus asleep with a partially eaten bundle of food beside her.

He sat and quietly started to eat. After a few minutes Mary opened her eyes and smiled. She told him about Rachel's visit, and Joseph relayed his experience at the inn and the synagogue. "God

Mary, the Lord's Servant

is so good," Joseph summarized. "And the tax collector briefly mentioned that a carpenter is needed around here. I think I can find some work to do so we can stay here for a time after the town is emptied of those who are here to register. That should be in just a few more days. Do you suppose that the Messiah should be raised in Bethlehem, the city of David? We will just need to follow the Lord's leading in this along with all other things."

The time slid by quickly as the new family got some much-needed rest. Both donkeys were given fresh hay and water. For the most part it was a quiet day except only occasionally when the baby awakened and demanded to be fed or tended to. Mary spread the baby's wet cloths on the stalls' wooden dividers, knowing that soon she would need to be settled elsewhere because those cloths and her own would need to be washed.

About mid-afternoon, Rachel returned. "I have wonderful news. The couple staying in our house would like to visit briefly before they travel to Jerusalem tonight, so you can come to our guest room and not spend another night in the stable."

"Oh, that would be wonderful," Mary replied. And behind Rachel appeared the couple, who approached Mary, Joseph, and the baby and indeed rejoiced with them at the birth of Jesus and all his birth meant.

After a short visit, they promised, "We will certainly tell our neighbors that the Messiah has come. May God guide you in all things and give you His peace." With that they left and Rachel followed them, telling Mary and Joseph she would be back shortly to escort them up the path to her house. Joseph gathered their things into the cart and was prepared to move by the time Rachel returned. Mary carried the baby, still snugly wrapped, to their new, temporary home.

CHAPTER EIGHT

PUZZLING WORDS IN JERUSALEM

Nathan and Rachel's home was small, only slightly larger than Mary and Joseph's home in Nazareth. It was also made of stones with a thick plaster holding the stones in place. It was a well-built home, Joseph noted. Rachel had been right — the guest room was quite small as it was not often occupied by guests. Usually it served as a storage area for the family. What Rachel had not mentioned to them yet was that they had two children, an active four-year-old son, Asa, and a six-month-old daughter, Elisheba. The house was clean and warmed by a hearth in the main room. Off to the side, separated by a partition only, was the guest room. The family sleeping room was behind the wall of the hearth so that it would also be warmed by a small fire in the hearth on cold winter nights.

Mary gratefully followed Rachel's instructions to settle into their small sleeping area, just barely wide enough for Mary and Joseph to sleep side by side. Mary made a baby's bed from blankets she had brought. Rachel warmed water on a small fire in the hearth and washed all the cloths that Mary had intended to wash, along with those she needed to wash for her own daughter. They just barely had time to get settled and eat a light evening meal when Joseph left to walk to the synagogue to join in the celebration of the Sabbath. Since there were still several visitors in the town because of the census, Joseph found himself blending in with visitors and townspeople in celebrating the Sabbath. Mary would not be allowed to attend the synagogue meetings until after her purification rites in Jerusalem, so Rachel decided to stay at the house with her and the children.

Only as the reading of the Prophets and the Law began did Nathan enter the synagogue and join the crowd. At the conclusion, he walked toward his home, recognized Joseph in the departing crowd, and realized they were walking toward the same destination. Nathan was surprised that he had new guests at his house, and now he was hosting the one whom the angels had announced. He was beyond delighted and rejoiced that his wife had been able to arrange the improvement in Joseph and Mary's housing.

Nathan announced he would be going back to the field after the Sabbath to lead his flock to their winter quarters, the stable cave just happily vacated by Mary and Joseph. There would be room for Joseph's donkey along with his, but it would be a crowded stable, and every day the sheep would be led only a short distance to feed on the winter's diminished grasses near Bethlehem. But at least at night the flock would be more protected in the approaching winter months from wolves and other predators that were more desperate and aggressive in securing food.

In the week ahead, the two families learned more about each other. Almost all the residents of Bethlehem were of the tribe of Judah, but not many were descendants of David, beloved king of Israel more than 1,000 years earlier. Joseph was a descendant of David through David's son Solomon. Nathan could trace his lineage back to David through David's son Nathan, as did Mary's father. Rachel and Nathan were delighted to have this couple, also of royal lineage, to share their home.

Joseph and Mary were interested to learn that the sheep Nathan raised were sold by vendors at the Temple for sacrifice for those who could not or did not bring a required lamb for their sacrificial offering. These lambs had to be perfect, without blemish as the Law required. Yet the hills where the sheep grazed were littered with many rocks and potential hazards that would cause disqualifications as sacrificial lambs. To prevent injuries, when a lamb was born, its legs were wrapped in strips of cloth. It was significant to the shepherds, therefore, when the angels announced that the new baby, the Messiah, the Savior of the world, would be found wrapped in swaddling cloths. Were the angels comparing the new baby to a lamb? A sacrificial lamb? How was the Messiah to be a sacrificial lamb and yet a conqueror? These questions remained unanswered.

When the baby was eight days old, even though it was the Sabbath, Mary and Joseph took the baby to the synagogue, where the rabbi circumcised him, and they named him Jesus as the angel had instructed both of them.

The shepherds' words about what they had seen and heard continued to be talked about in the town of Bethlehem. As in Nazareth, some were excited and believed; others did not.

The information that Joseph was a builder made the rounds, and a few asked him to repair various items. Then Micah, the innkeeper, approached him about adding another large room to the inn. Micah was buoyed by the profits from the influx of guests during the census even though he knew that most of his customers were merchants that traveled the road between Jerusalem and Hebron and other places south and west, including Egypt. Joseph was grateful to begin an extended job that would generate income for his family.

Joseph had a good start on the project when the time came, forty days after Jesus' birth, to travel to Jerusalem for Mary's purification rites and Jesus' presentation to the Lord. In accordance to the Law of Moses, "every firstborn male is to be consecrated to the Lord." Mary and Joseph were required by the Law to offer a sacrifice of "two turtledoves or two young pigeons." This was the least expensive offering. Others who were wealthier offered a more expensive gift such as a lamb. Joseph was thankful that because of his recent work they would be able to afford to buy the two turtledoves at the Temple.

Joseph informed Micah, the innkeeper, of their upcoming travel to Jerusalem, which actually would not take more than two days if they returned immediately to Bethlehem. But Joseph wanted to please Mary by asking for more time to be gone so they could make the extra trip on to Ein Kerem to visit with Zechariah and Elizabeth and meet their seven-month-old son, John. Now that the census was complete, the town was emptied of the many visitors. Micah was not anticipating any extra guests in the upcoming months and was comfortable with Joseph suspending his building project for a week.

When Joseph told Mary of his arrangement with Micah and the plan to visit Elizabeth and Zechariah, she was overjoyed. She desired very strongly to pour into her soul the presence of the Spirit that she felt at her cousin's house. So Joseph secured his tools and belongings they would not need in the upcoming days, and they departed early in the morning forty days after Jesus' birth.

Their trip to Jerusalem was much easier than it had been going the other direction just less than six weeks earlier. The day was cool, which made for good travel. They led the donkey in case Mary needed to ride for a while, but for most of the five-mile trip Mary walked, sometimes carrying Jesus. Joseph also loved to carry this new life. It was so good to move around, but Mary realized she was not completely back to full strength. Just outside of Jerusalem, they went a short distance away from the road to a more secluded spot to tend to the baby's needs as Joseph shielded them from view. Then they entered Jerusalem.

Puzzling Words in Jerusalem

Mary was excited! Of the recent times she had been in and through Jerusalem, she had not had the opportunity to enter the Temple courts and observe and join in with other worshippers. Joseph secured the donkey in a designated area to the south of the Temple walls, and they walked up the southern steps into the Temple grounds. Mary and Joseph first noticed the Pharisees and Sadducees in their fine ornamented robes and headdresses. Some were occupied with prayers and worship, others carefully watched the crowds.

Many people milled about the large plaza that had just in the past twenty years been expanded to thirty-two acres by King Herod's builders. The large stones of the Temple court's outer walls that had been mined and prepared in a quarry just outside of the city walls were so finely chiseled that no mortar was needed to fit them tightly together. The magnificent Temple that housed the Holy Place and the Holy of Holies stood tall above them in beautiful marble. Gold overlay on the columns gleamed in the sun. Work continued on the outer areas, such as the many tall columns and roof of what was called Solomon's Porch, where people would gather in later years to worship God and discuss the Word of God. Along the entire south wall of the Temple complex would be the magnificent Royal Portico, which would take many more years to complete. The pungent scent of the morning sacrifice that had been offered on the altar in front of the Temple still lingered in the air. Additional offerings were being prepared to the north of the altar.

Joseph first went to the money changers to exchange a small amount of money from the Roman coins into the Temple (Jewish) money. He and Mary then approached a seller of doves. *Should they be right here on these new Temple grounds?* wondered Joseph. Next they needed to locate a priest on duty to ask him to offer the sacrifice of the two doves required by the Law of Moses, one for a burnt offering and the other for the purification offering. When they had finally fulfilled these tasks, they slowly walked around the

Mary, the Lord's Servant

courtyard for several minutes just soaking up the glorious atmosphere of this holy House of God, rejoicing again in Jesus' birth.

Mary was allowed to approach the Temple itself only as far as the Court of Women. Joseph left Jesus in his mother's care as he entered the Court of Men to offer a prayer of thanksgiving and a petition for guidance in raising this new, holy child.

Afterward Joseph rejoined Mary, and they left the Court of Women. They had entered the larger, outside court, the Court of the Gentiles, when they were approached by an elderly man. He obviously was overjoyed to see them although they did not know him. He introduced himself as Simeon and declared that the Holy Spirit had revealed to him that he would not die until he had seen the Lord's Messiah. That day the Spirit had led him to the Temple and then specifically to Joseph, Mary and the baby — he knew that the prophecy given him had come to pass. When he reached out to take Jesus from Mary's arms, she surrendered the baby to him. He lifted Jesus up and praised God, saying, "Sovereign Lord, now let your servant die in peace, as you have promised. I have seen your salvation, which you have prepared for all people. He is a light to reveal God to the nations, and he is the glory of your people Israel!"

Jesus' parents were amazed at what was being said about him. Simeon blessed them, and then turning to Mary, he prophesied, "This child is destined to cause many in Israel to fall, but he will be a joy to many others. He has been sent as a sign from God, but many will oppose him. As a result, the deepest thoughts of many hearts will be revealed. And a sword will pierce your very soul."

His words stunned and puzzled Joseph and Mary. ". . . Cause many in Israel to fall"? ... "Many will oppose him"? How could he say this about the Messiah? What sort of prophecy was this? He had said, "A sword will pierce your very soul," while looking directly at Mary. What could that mean? But they didn't have time to sort it out quite yet.

Puzzling Words in Jerusalem

As Simeon was talking, an elderly woman approached them at that very moment. She began praising God, confirming that what Simeon had said was from the Lord. Anna, as she introduced herself, had been praying night and day at the Temple for many years. She was now eighty-four, she said! She never left the Temple and fasted and worshiped there. Many heads turned and people crowded near to hear what Anna had to say. She obviously was known and respected by those in the Temple. She blessed the baby and Mary and Joseph, then sent them on their way. As they made their way through the crowd gathering around Anna, they heard her proclaim to all who were waiting expectantly for God to rescue Jerusalem that the Messiah, the Redeemer, had been born.

As Mary and Joseph walked toward Ein Kerem, they were puzzled about what had just happened at the Temple. Mary sat on the donkey to cradle Jesus as he slept. She pushed all these events into her heart to think about and relive them in her memory in the upcoming days, even years.

They arrived at Zechariah and Elizabeth's home in mid-afternoon and knocked on the courtyard gate. Shortly Carmen opened the gate, and a wide smile spread over her face. "Come in, come in!" she welcomed them. Joseph helped Mary dismount while still holding the sleeping Jesus. Walking by was a young boy Carmen knew, and she called to him, asking him to take the donkey to the stables located around back, promising him a shekel or two. He was eager to do as requested.

Hearing noises in the courtyard, Zechariah came out of the house to the wonderful surprise that had arrived. Silent no more, his joyous voice welcomed them. He quickly ushered them into the house to greet Elizabeth. As they were warmly and joyously welcomed by Elizabeth and Zechariah, the happiness doubled when each couple met the other's son. John was a much-loved, active, obviously intelligent baby. Jesus slept through the introductions. The two families settled comfortably into the main living space

Mary, the Lord's Servant

to visit as Carmen was instructed to first wash their feet and then prepare the best guest room.

As Joseph was introduced to Elizabeth and Zechariah, Mary asked him to tell the older couple about how the angel had appeared to him in a dream and how he made sure Mary was accepted as his wife the very next day. Zechariah and Elizabeth rejoiced in hearing these details and welcomed Joseph as part of the family. Joseph immediately loved the much older couple and reveled in their spiritual depths. Elizabeth could easily see why Mary had loved Joseph from the start and realized God had placed them together so that they could raise the Son of God. That evening Mary and Joseph told them about the angel's visit to the shepherds and then the host of angels that appeared to them, praising God. They recounted their current stay in Bethlehem as well. They again all rejoiced at God's marvelous workings in their lives and went to bed tired but full of joy at the Spirit's work in their families.

It wasn't until the next day that Joseph and Mary described the events at the Temple for Zechariah and Elizabeth, telling them of the words of Simeon and Anna. "Yes," Zechariah agreed. "I know both of them to be filled with the Spirit of God. It does not surprise me that Simeon had a prophecy for you and that Anna was drawn to you." Suddenly, the elderly Zechariah practically jumped up and said, "I have something to show to you," as he hurried from the room. He stopped in the doorway, turned around, and corrected himself, "No, to give to you."

Mary and Joseph looked at each other surprised as Elizabeth just said, "Oh, you will want to see this."

Zechariah returned shortly with a rolled-up parchment and carefully unrolled it on the table before them. "I recorded what the angel said to me in the Temple when he told me about our prayers for a child being answered. I also have written as carefully as I could what you, Mary, told us about the angel's visit to you and his words. And I have written what Elizabeth and you spoke by the power of the Holy Spirit when your father brought you to our house. What you don't know is that when John was born, I was not able to speak until eight days later when he was to be circumcised and was to be named. Everyone around us wanted to name him Zechariah, but Elizabeth kept insisting, 'No! His name is John!' Confused because no one in our family had that name, they asked me what I would like to name the child. I asked for a writing tablet and to everyone's surprise I wrote, 'His name is John.' Immediately I could speak again and began praising God.

"Then I too prophesied by the Holy Spirit, and I have written down what I said:

> Praise the Lord, the God of Israel, because he has visited and redeemed his people. He has sent us a mighty Savior from the royal line of his servant David, just as he promised through his holy prophets long ago. Now we will be saved from our enemies and from all who hate us. He has been merciful to our ancestors by remembering his sacred covenant — the covenant he swore with an oath to our ancestor Abraham. We have been rescued from our enemies so we can serve God without fear, in holiness and righteousness for as long as we live.

> And you, my little son, will be called the prophet of the Most High, because you will prepare the way for the Lord. You will tell his people how to find salvation through forgiveness of their sins. Because of God's tender mercy, the morning light from heaven is about to break upon us, to give light to those who sit in darkness and in the shadow of death, and to guide us to the path of peace."

Mary, the Lord's Servant

Zechariah finished reading his prophecy and laid the parchment on the table.

He described the results. "When I first said this, awe fell upon the whole neighborhood, and the news of what happened has spread throughout the Judean hills. Everyone who heard about it has reflected on these events and asks, 'What will this child turn out to be?' For the hand of the Lord is surely upon him in a special way."

Zechariah re-rolled the parchment and handed it to Joseph. "Please keep this," he said, "and write on it what you heard from the angel in your dream, what the shepherds heard and saw, and what Simeon and Anna told you at the Temple yesterday. It will bring you great encouragement and will help you through any difficult times that may come. Keep it only to yourself. I doubt you should share it with others."

Joseph gratefully accepted the parchment. "Yes, I will. Thank you so very much. In fact, if you will help me, I will do that while we are here." Of course Zechariah readily consented to the plan.

The remaining four days with Zechariah and Elizabeth flew by as Joseph and Mary continued to soak in the Spirit of the Lord and encouragement from them. The days included spending a Sabbath with them and attending the local synagogue. Joseph and Mary observed the respect and honor that the elderly couple and their baby received from the people of the village. Then Joseph knew he must return to Bethlehem and continue his work on the inn expansion room.

As they prepared to depart, Zechariah held their hands and blessed them:

May the Lord bless you and protect you.
May the Lord smile on you and be gracious to you.
May the Lord show you his favor and give you his peace.

CHAPTER NINE

ROYAL VISITORS

Back in Bethlehem, Joseph discovered he needed assistance in several ways, and Micah gladly hired help for Joseph to move the building project on more quickly. Micah had grown to appreciate the skills and dedication to his craft that Joseph exhibited in the excellence of the construction.

In a matter of a few months, the inn addition was completed except for the waterproofing of the roof, which would need to be done during the olive harvest in a couple of months. Joseph had mentioned to Micah about using a different type of roofing, a mix of clay and straw, but it did not last as long as the olive pulp waterproofing. Some wealthier homes had roofs of clay tile, but Micah had opted not to go to that expense at this time. As Joseph waited for the time of the olive harvest to arrive, his reputation brought him several other projects, although thankfully they were smaller. He was happy to be kept busy and to have the income.

As winter's crisp air gave way to the promise of spring, Mary thought often about the coming Passover celebration. She hoped that when Joseph returned he would bring her father and perhaps her mother with him for a visit. Then news arrived in Bethlehem of a rebellion in Galilee. A group of rebels led by a Galilean named Judas had attacked the Roman garrison at Sepphoris. The leader was killed and his followers scattered, but this led to an increased

Mary, the Lord's Servant

Roman presence in Galilee, including in Nazareth. It was unknown whether anyone from the area would be allowed to make the journey to Jerusalem for Passover.

When Joseph and Nathan returned from the celebration, they reported only Rabbi James and ten older men had come from Nazareth. The others had to remain in the village. Mary was concerned for her family's safety, certainly, but could not deny her disappointment in not being able to introduce her three-month-old son to his grandparents.

In the following months, Jesus began to crawl as he played with Asa and Elisheba. Mary's friendship with Rachel also deepened, and they developed a sister-bond. When winter had passed, Nathan returned to the field to lead the sheep to better pastures. His flock grew, and he carefully cared for the lambs, knowing that many of them would be sold to be sacrificial lambs at the Temple in Jerusalem. He only occasionally made his way home as his hired helpers watched the flock. When he was home, Rachel prepared as much "away from home" food as she could for him. Mary helped by taking care of the children while Rachel was busy preparing food.

Summer passed into fall and indeed the olive harvest began. Joseph had an agreement with a local olive grove owner to purchase the pulp after the third press although Joseph had to walk almost halfway to Jerusalem to procure it. Joseph's little cart pulled by the donkey worked well, but they had to move as quickly as possible to get the pulp to the roof of the inn addition before the pulp dried. He had to make several trips to accomplish it, but by mid-fall the project was completed. Micah and Ethlan were thrilled with Joseph's work and their expanded inn, anticipating even more customers to stay there.

Elisheba was six months older than Jesus, and he had watched her learn to walk. He now had begun pulling himself up using

Royal Visitors

whatever was available. Joseph and Mary reveled in Jesus' growth and enjoyed every moment they could spend with him.

Just a few days before Jesus' first birthday, a great commotion stirred in Jerusalem. A large, wealthy group of travelers entered the gates of Jerusalem, obviously on their way to visit King Herod. Soon the city was abuzz with the news of the visitors' arrival, and spectators gathered along the route to King Herod's palace, which was located in the western part of Jerusalem. Micah had gone to the city that day and made his way to the front of the crowd so he could see what was happening. Servants dressed in bright colors of silk clothing were leading the camels, ten of which had tall travel boxes fixed on their backs, highly decorated with silky fabrics that those in Jerusalem had rarely seen. Richly ornamented tassels hung from the camels' halters and the blankets covering their backs. The fabrics of the travel boxes were drawn back to reveal men dressed even more elaborately than their servants who were guiding the camels. The men wore bejeweled crowns of gold. The parade of fifteen camels slowly made its way toward King Herod's palace. A crowd of curious onlookers gathered outside the palace as news filtered from inside the palace, telling the story of what was happening there.

King Herod had received word of the travelers' impending arrival as they approached Jerusalem and was prepared to receive them with honor although he did not know the reason for their visit. He knew in advance that they had come from the east, probably the Persian area, also part of the Roman Empire, and were advisors — called Magi, or wise men — to the king there as had been the tradition for centuries in Persia. But the reason for their visit remained a mystery.

King Herod welcomed the esteemed visitors into his throne room with pomp to show his royal status. The Magi bowed to the King and promptly asked, "Where is the newborn king of the Jews? We saw his star as it rose, and we have come to worship him."

Mary, the Lord's Servant

King Herod was deeply disturbed when he heard this. The news of the Magi's first words was quickly reported to the crowd outside the palace, along with King Herod's reaction. This news spread quickly across the city, causing many to be worried. What did these wise men from eastern lands mean? A King of the Jews had been born? These men knew this because they had seen a star? What would King Herod's response be to this information?

Then Micah and the assembled crowd waiting outside the palace heard more reports of the further conversation of the visitors. It seems these wise men studied the stars and made predictions for their king from their observations. In summary, they had observed the star that represented royalty as it lined up with the star that represented the Israelite nation. It was an event of great significance and had made a strong impact on them and on their Persian king. Their king had given them permission to prepare for and make this trip to Jerusalem, the capital city of the nation of Israel, to worship this great one whose birth had been announced in the heavens. It had taken almost six months of careful preparation and six months of laborious travel to reach their destination. Now they desired to worship this new king.

King Herod invited his royal visitors, the Magi, to rest from their journey in the comfort of an adjoining room as he ordered a rich array of refreshments for them.

Then King Herod quickly sent for the leading priests and teachers of religious law to come without delay to the palace. He knew no baby had been born in his own family for many years. Thirty-three years earlier, the Roman Senate had appointed him as king of Judea. A new Jewish king would be a tragedy for his rule. The Romans would descend with a fury if anyone tried to usurp their authority and re-establish the autonomy of the Jewish nation. Several had tried to start a revolt against Rome, and each one had been defeated and destroyed. But this was a different situation. It had been announced in the stars! King Herod knew enough about

Royal Visitors

the Jewish Laws and Prophets to know that one called the Messiah, one who was to be the Christ, the Redeemer of the Israelite people, was prophesied to come to the Israelite nation.

The chief priests and teachers of the Law had already heard of the Magi's arrival and were informed of their disturbing question. Herod had been pacing the room and quickly asked as the priests and teachers entered, "Where is the Messiah supposed to be born?" This was a different question than the Magi had asked.

The pinpoint question almost caught the chief priests by surprise, and they looked alarmed at each other. Then the Chief High Priest Annas replied for all of them: "In Bethlehem in Judea, for this is what the prophet [Micah] wrote: 'And you, O Bethlehem in the land of Judah, are not least among the ruling cities of Judah, for a ruler will come from you who will be the shepherd for my people Israel.'" Then trying to calm King Herod's fears, Annas added, "Bethlehem is a small, inconsequential town. I doubt the Magi will find our Messiah there," although Annas did not remind King Herod that Israel's great King David had been born in Bethlehem and, yes, the Messiah would be born there, too. *Would it be, could it be, now?* he wondered.

King Herod requested the Magi to rejoin him in the throne room. Although they had rested only a couple of hours, they were anxious to continue on their journey if the new king of the Jews was not to be found in this palace. The Magi were greeted again by King Herod, who with a sweep of his hand indicated the leaders of the Jewish religion. "These men have informed me that the King of the Jews, the Christ, is to be born in Bethlehem. It is a small town just five miles south of our great capital city." With that he dismissed the religious leaders and all his own advisors from the room. When the room cleared except for the Magi, he asked them to approach his throne and inquired, "Tell me about this star. When did you see it?"

Mary, the Lord's Servant

The Magi answered, "Almost a year ago. We eagerly look forward to finding this child."

King Herod told them, "Go to Bethlehem and search carefully for the child. And when you find him, come back and tell me so that I can go and worship him, too."

The sun was setting by the time the Magi were once again on their way. They didn't mind traveling in the dark since their servants ahead carried torches to light the way and the Magi could see the stars as they traveled. They were overjoyed when the bright star they had seen months before appeared again in the sky. Using their instruments of astronomy, they could tell it was guiding them toward Bethlehem.

Micah had hurried home as soon as he heard that the Magi were to go to Bethlehem. He hoped this meant that he would have these royal advisors as guests at his inn that very night. In his mind he was thinking, "This certainly would certify that the child Jesus is indeed the Messiah, the Savior, as the shepherds had said angels told them almost a year ago." As Micah arrived at his inn, he informed his wife of all that he had learned in Jerusalem that day and instructed her to prepare their new, large addition for the likelihood of hosting the royal travelers. He then hurried to Nathan's house to inform him and his house guests that they may be visited by these Magi. As the following events unfolded, Nathan was glad that his sheep were already in the cave below and he was at home. Joseph was glad they had moved the donkeys to the front of the stable cave.

Mary and Joseph, along with Nathan and Rachel, were once again amazed at what God was doing as Micah told them about the Magi making their way toward Bethlehem. What were they to do? Just wait, they decided. It was past the children's bedtimes, but the parents decided they should not yet put the children to bed since they would more than likely be disturbed and reawakened shortly. As the exclamations of the villagers indicated that the visitors were

Royal Visitors

approaching, they left the house to stand outside. Villagers came out of their houses with eyes wide at the very unusual sight.

Soon the richly robed foreigners entered the village gates and stopped. The man on the lead camel held the large instrument used to study the stars in his arms and lifted it to show the others behind him. The bright star was almost directly above, but the instrument indicated they needed to go a short distance into the village, which they did. When the star stopped, they came to a halt in front of Nathan and Rachel's house.

The large traveling group filled the narrow street of the village as they crowded as close together as they could. The camels were made to kneel and the servants placed a step beside each of the boxes affixed to the camels. The Magi in rich array and crowns alighted from their perches. One of them, an older man, stepped forward and slightly bowed to Nathan, Rachel, Joseph and Mary, who was holding Jesus in her arms. The visitor spoke in Greek, the common language of the Roman Empire, stating the purpose of their visit. "We seek the baby born King of the Jews." Nathan nodded and indicated the child Mary was holding. The one who spoke immediately turned his attention to Jesus and bowed low on one knee right there in the street! The other nine Magi came forward, bowing low before Jesus. Such a holy and awesome moment! A shockwave of holiness spread over all the visitors, Magi and servants alike, and all those who witnessed this were awed.

Again, the first Magi spoke, "May we come into the house?"

Joseph looked at the large number, and nodded, wondering how they were all going to fit into the small space inside. Mary and Joseph led the visitors inside, and Mary sat holding Jesus, who was quiet; the bright clothing of the visitors captured and held his attention.

Then Mary spoke to the crowded room. "Yes, this is Jesus, the Messiah, proclaimed to me by an angel and announced by angels

Mary, the Lord's Servant

to shepherds the night of his birth. Several prophesies and other signs have been given to confirm this to us as well."

The lead Magi spoke again, "We have traveled far after seeing a sign in the stars indicating that the King of the Jews had been born. We were urged by what we saw nearly a year ago to come to worship the new king. We are familiar with your holy writings since descendants of your ancestors remain in our country. We knew the coming of this King is significant for all people. The star we saw when we were in the east appeared again tonight to lead us from Jerusalem to Bethlehem to this child. It is a joy to worship him and to complete the mission of our journey."

There was no room for the servants to enter the house along with the Magi, so from the doorway, servants handed treasure chests to their masters, who presented gifts as they jostled to approach one by one, and once again to kneel before Jesus. "Please accept our gifts of gold, frankincense, and myrrh." Mary and Joseph were almost speechless but graciously accepted the gifts meant for a king.

For several quiet minutes the Magi continued to kneel in worship of the one they had identified as the King of the Jews before they slowly left the house, awed by the completion of their long journey in this humble abode. They returned to their kneeling camels and prepared to remount.

Micah carefully approached one of the Magi, bowed and asked, "Would you spend the night at my inn? We have a wonderful new room that would accommodate your entire party."

The man smiled at the innkeeper but shook his head. "We have slept in the open for the past six months and have all that we need for a good night's rest. We will find an open field just outside of town to make our camp. Thank you for letting us know of your inn, but we will not need to stay there."

Mary and Joseph stared at each other as their visitors left, silently conveying to each other their wonder at what had occurred. Nathan and Rachel came into the room as it cleared of its visitors and were as awestruck as Mary and Joseph were. These royal visitors traveled for six months to worship Jesus! Where would all this lead? Would this change the Roman domination of their country? How would this child become Israel's Redeemer? Now that God had made Jesus' birth even more public, how would the Romans react? What about King Herod?

Thankfully the villagers had returned to their own homes to discuss the astounding events of the evening. Why had the Magi come from a long distance to, as they said, "worship the king of the Jews"? Did this go along with the shepherds' insistence that angels had spoken to them about this child almost a year ago? Many of them fully intended to call a meeting at the synagogue the following day to hear the Magi's words that were spoken to Joseph and Mary. But for now they would discuss it among themselves and get a good night's sleep.

Mary laid sleepy Jesus down for the night. Rachel was doing the same for her two children. Nathan and Joseph walked to the backyard and talked about the amazing event, again wondering what path was ahead for Mary and Joseph as they raised Jesus. God had used the superstitions of these foreign astrologers, the meanings they assigned to various celestial events, plus their knowledge of Jewish Scriptures to fulfill His purposes. These noble Gentiles traveled months to worship a Jewish Messiah and give him royal gifts!

With all this on their minds, Mary and Joseph retired to their sleeping room and as they lay next to each other, spoke in low voices so they wouldn't awaken Jesus. They wondered why God would send gold, frankincense, and myrrh. What would they do with these rich gifts? Finally, Joseph whispered, "This is definitely something I will add to the parchment that Zechariah gave me."

Just a few hours later in the darkness of night, Joseph urgently shook Mary awake. "Mary, we must leave this place immediately! An angel has appeared to me in a dream. He said, 'Get up! Flee to

Mary, the Lord's Servant

Egypt with the child and his mother. Stay there until I tell you to return, because Herod is going to search for the child to kill him.'"

"Oh, no!" Mary cried. "Now? We must leave now?"

"Yes, now!" Joseph replied. His voice reflected the gravity of the angel's message. They quickly and quietly made plans. Joseph would go get the donkey from the stable below and bring it up to the back of the house where the cart was stored. He would first load his tools into the cart. Mary would light a lamp from the hearth's dying embers and fold blankets and clothes, ready to add them to the cart. Mary would ride the donkey, carrying Jesus, hoping he would continue to sleep.

As Joseph left the house and Mary began gathering their few belongings, she heard Rachel's voice, "Mary? Is something wrong?"

"Yes! An angel spoke to Joseph in a dream and told him that we must leave right now because King Herod is going to try to find Jesus to kill him!" Mary's voice trembled.

Rachel understood the gravity and urgency of the angel's warning. King Herod had already killed two of his sons and one of his wives out of jealousy for his throne. He certainly had been made aware of Jesus and that he had been born in Bethlehem. Yes, he definitely was capable of trying to eliminate another perceived threat to his throne.

"Let me help you, Mary. I will gather up a bit of food for you to take with you," Rachel offered.

"That would be so generous. Oh ..." Mary hesitated in her hurry. "I hate to have to leave this way. Your kindness has been so wonderful ..." Rachel quickly hugged Mary and rushed to gather some food for the departing family.

Joseph came in the door and picked up belongings to be added to the cart, including the amazing treasures given to them by the Magi only a few hours before. Blankets and clothes provided coverage for the contents of the cart, but now the cart was heavier than it had been when they first came. Oh, so much had changed in the past year!

CHAPTER TEN

A NEW CITY

"We must go now," Joseph said to Nathan, who had awakened to the shocking news. "We don't have time for long goodbyes, but you have been like family to us. Thank you so much." Nathan hugged Joseph as Mary picked up the nearly-one-year-old Jesus. He stirred and whimpered, but Mary gently said, "Shhhhh, child," and he relaxed in her arms.

Mary decided to straddle the donkey for better balance while holding Jesus, so Joseph put a blanket over Jesus that also covered and warmed Mary's legs. Then as quietly as possible, they left for Egypt, heading down the street, through Bethlehem's city gate, and toward the main road.

The moon shone just enough light for them to safely travel down the hill leaving Bethlehem. The road going south toward Hebron and on to Egypt branched to the left, and they began their journey down the unfamiliar path. They traveled in silence for a couple of hours, escaping with the Son of God, the Messiah, no doubt guarded by angels.

Joseph led the donkey with a long rope so he could also pull the cart. After they crested a slight hill, he could see a grove of trees just off the road. "Mary," he said quietly, "I think we should finish the night under those trees. Jesus will sleep. The sun will be up in a couple of hours, and we can continue then."

Mary nodded. Her arms were tired from holding Jesus and trying to buffer the motions of the donkey to make it a gentle ride for the sleeping child.

Joseph found an easy place to leave the road, and they went a short distance into the grove of trees. Although the trees made it even darker, they found a good spot to rest. They settled in, and the donkey immediately laid down to rest. Just as daybreak was adding more light, they heard soldiers moving swiftly along the road Mary and Joseph had just traveled, and sure enough they crested the hill. Mary felt sure the loud pounding of her heart would give them away. Joseph couldn't see the men, and apparently the soldiers didn't see the family, because the soldiers rode on. Joseph whispered, "O Lord our God, thank you. Please continue to protect us."

Mary found the food that Rachel had hastily wrapped for them and ate a little, and as Jesus awoke Mary fed and tended to him. Just a half hour after they had heard the soldiers the first time, going south, they heard them return, going north. *Were the soldiers searching for them?* Thankfully, they didn't spot the frightened family. The little family was only about five miles south of Bethlehem and their journey to Egypt would take many days, perhaps two weeks or more. They would find some towns along the way, but not many, especially when they traveled through the northern part of the Sinai Desert.

After waiting and resting a short time longer, Joseph decided it was safe to travel again so they started out, first with Joseph carrying Jesus, and Mary leading the donkey, who was pulling the cart. After a couple of hours, Joseph had an idea. He shaped the blankets in the top of the cart to form a bowl and placed the child there. Jesus thought it was a great place to travel, so Mary walked beside him, and Joseph led the donkey. By late afternoon they neared Hebron and found an inn there. Joseph unloaded the cart, being careful not to let the gifts of the Magi be seen under the blankets as he carried them in. The inn had good food, and Jesus charmed the innkeeper's

A New City

wife with his cherub face and smile. Joseph and Mary were grateful for the good rest they got that night.

As they left Hebron early the following morning, they passed the gravesite of Abraham, Isaac, Jacob and their wives. King Herod had recently built an ornate wall to encircle the Cave of the Patriarchs. This was the first time Joseph and Mary had been this far south, and although they knew they should not linger, they spent a few moments in front of the notable site honoring their ancestors.

The journey to Egypt was long. The merchants' road took them south to Beersheba, then west toward the Mediterranean Sea, along the Besor Brook. Thankfully, this road was somewhat shaded by the trees that grew along the brook. Some nights they found refuge in a town, and many nights they spent under the stars.

Most of the other travelers were merchants going to or coming from Egypt. Joseph and Mary never felt unsafe; they knew God's protection was over them. As they traveled, Joseph and Mary encouraged each other by quoting God's promises to each other, many from the Psalms. One of Mary's favorites was from a song of David:

> As for me, I will sing about your power.
> Each morning I will sing with joy about your
>   unfailing love.
> For you have been my refuge, a place of safety when I
>   am in distress.
> O my Strength, to you I sing praises, for you, O God, are
>   my refuge,
> the God who shows me unfailing love.

Then the road went along the Mediterranean Sea toward Egypt. At Raphia, the innkeeper recommended to them that they travel the road across the hot desert at night, which they did, making a shelter to rest under during the day. Finally, they arrived at the border of

Mary, the Lord's Servant

Egypt, rejoicing they had traveled a difficult distance safely with a young child.

After following the road another two days, they arrived at another river. Since this was a wider and deeper river, a large boat ferried them and the donkey across the river, and they found themselves in a strange city, Alexandria. The houses, the people's clothing, the smells of food cooking — it was all so different than that to which they had been accustomed. They knew they needed first to find a place to live. Joseph had been praying for guidance as they approached the city. They first selected a place that was serving food. They relaxed a bit when they discovered that because the Romans had conquered Egypt also, the common trade language was Greek, and the currency was Roman coins.

The chatty food vendor was kind and struck up a conversation with Joseph. When Joseph returned to Mary, he said, "God led us here. This food vendor, Naphron, knows where we can rent a house. There is a large settlement of others from Israel. Naphron will take us there when his son arrives to take over the shop in an hour."

Before long Naphron was guiding Mary and Joseph down many streets, some paved in the more affluent areas of town, some just sandy dirt. At last they came to a small neighborhood away from the busyness of the main parts of the city. Mary and Joseph were introduced to a man named Eliakim, leader of the Jewish community there, who knew of a small house where the newcomers could stay. The house fit Mary and Joseph's needs perfectly. Eliakim returned to their house a few days later to check on them, and before long they were friends. They made acquaintances with their neighbors and continued to seek the Lord from day to day.

Eliakim made sure they knew where the synagogue was, and Mary and Joseph relished their fellowship with these Jewish descendants of those who had translated the precious Word of God from Hebrew into Greek. This translation, called the Septuagint, was being used in many places so that Jews and non-Jews alike could

A New City

learn the history of the Jews, the Laws of Moses and the Prophets. Although the Jews in Alexandria had accepted and adopted many of the Greek-influenced ways, they believed firmly in the God of Israel.

Eliakim was also the source of news. He told them the horrific story that had arrived by way of a merchant who had traveled through Bethlehem. Some royal visitors claimed to have seen a child they identified as the King of the Jews. They had camped overnight just outside of town, but by morning they were gone, their campsite mysteriously emptied. Mary and Joseph smiled inwardly at the story until Eliakim continued.

The visitors' departure had angered King Herod, so he sent soldiers on a mission to find that child with orders to ensure his death by killing all the boys in and around Bethlehem who were two years old and under. Joseph and Mary's hearts ached when they heard this news. In the months they spent in Bethlehem, they had made acquaintances with several families that had boys who must have been included in this slaughter. How those families must be hurting! What a cruel thing for King Herod to have done! They knew that God had warned Joseph at the right moment, and they had escaped just in time. That explained why they had heard the soldiers that early morning after leaving Bethlehem. Evidently the soldiers had ridden as far as they thought the family could have gone. The second time Mary and Joseph heard them, the soldiers must have been returning toward Bethlehem or Jerusalem.

Joseph's funds ran low, but he could find no carpentry repair work, so Naphron connected Joseph to a seller of myrrh who was willing to purchase the myrrh from him. That money provided them rent and food for several months. Later they also had to sell the frankincense, again funding their living for another few months. Joseph had also begun to use the gold coins.

One day Mary caught Joseph by surprise. "Joseph, I think I am with child, your child."

Mary, the Lord's Servant

"What?" It was joyous news to Joseph. He loved Jesus with all his heart and desired to add more children to their family.

Shortly after that, after almost a year of living in Egypt, an angel of the Lord again appeared in a dream to Joseph. "Get up!" the angel said. "Take the child and his mother back to the land of Israel, because those who were trying to kill the child are dead."

Joseph and Mary rejoiced that they were to return to their home country. They said farewell to the friends they had made and prepared once again to travel. While in Egypt, Jesus had begun walking and talking. Their family dynamic would be changing as well with the arrival of another child in six months.

So Joseph and Mary traveled back to Israel. Another arduous journey — this time with an almost-two-year-old child. Their intention was to return to Bethlehem, the city of David, for since it was prophesied the Messiah would be born there, they reasoned that perhaps he was also to be raised there. Mary and Joseph had become close friends with Nathan and Rachel and looked forward to seeing them again. They would be able to visit with Elizabeth and Zechariah and John occasionally, so they traveled in that direction.

However, stopping overnight again in Raphia, they heard the news that Herod's son Archelaus was the new ruler of Judea. Joseph was told that Archelaus was as ruthless as his father had been, so Joseph was afraid to go there. As they retired for the evening at the Raphia inn, they discussed whether to go ahead and return to Bethlehem. They knew God had protected them to this point, and they trusted God to continue to protect them. They decided to retrace their route of the previous year on the road along the Besor Brook, going through Hebron and then north to Bethlehem. That night, however, Joseph had another dream in which he was warned not to return to Bethlehem. So again their plans changed.

The news they had heard also told them the area of Galilee — where Nazareth was — was under the rule of another of King Herod's sons, Herod Antipas. *Was God guiding them to return to*

A New City

their hometown? they wondered. Heeding the warning of the angel of the Lord, Mary and Joseph continued north on the road near the Mediterranean Sea, staying in or near towns such as Ascalon, Ashdod, Joppa, Caesarea, and Dora until they were south of Mount Carmel. They finally reached the road which would take them east through the Jezreel Valley and back to Nazareth.

They were extremely weary after more than two weeks of travel so they were elated when they once again saw Mount Precipice as they walked east past the fertile soil of the Jezreel Valley. Soon the winter barley and wheat would be planted. A gentle rain began to fall, the rain that was known as the early rain that prepared the soil for the seeds to be planted. Joseph picked up Jesus to shelter him as much as possible.

Late in the day, almost two years since they had departed Nazareth, they climbed the hill to their hometown. Again, it was Mary's younger brothers, Amos and Simon, who saw them first. The boys' cry of "Mary's home!" followed by joyous shouting and hollering brought Johanna running toward them. She hugged Mary first and then saw Joseph holding Jesus. With a grandmother's joyful heart, she drew in a breath. "So this is Jesus!" Jesus was not quite sure what the commotion was all about. He just wanted Joseph to put him down. He was tired of being carried. But as soon as he was on his own feet, his grandmother's hug enveloped him. She kissed him on the cheek and said to the whole family, "Welcome home."

EPILOGUE – 58 YEARS LATER

"EVERY KNEE WILL BOW"

Mary looked fondly at the old parchment unrolled before her. She had not revealed it to anyone until now, but Doctor Luke asked to interview her about Jesus' birth and ministry. Luke had been asked by a wealthy Roman believer named Theophilus to write an account of Jesus' birth, ministry, death, and resurrection. Although Luke was not an eyewitness to Jesus' ministry, he wanted to have precise information for this non-Jewish reader. A young man named Mark had already written the story of Jesus' life and ministry while talking with Peter, the disciple. Another disciple, Matthew, had mentioned he wanted to write the same story, but his focus would be on the Jews because he wanted to reference the many fulfilled prophecies about the Messiah. Mary had mentioned that she thought someday John, her nephew (also a disciple), may also record the good news about Jesus and his ministry. He was the youngest of the disciples — only fifteen years old when Jesus called him. But he could shed a lot of insight into Jesus' teachings since they had enjoyed such a close relationship.

Mary showed to Luke what had been written sixty years earlier on the parchment and talked with him for hours, telling him about Jesus' miraculous birth, their flight into Egypt, and eventual return to Nazareth. James had been added to the family just six months after their return, and in the next years, he was followed by Joseph,

Mary, the Lord's Servant

Judas (who prefers now to go by Jude), Simon, and their three sisters. It was a busy but happy household.

Jesus' early years had been a turbulent political time in the land of Israel as the Romans put down several Jewish revolts after the death of King Herod. Herod's kingdom had been divided among his children, but after only a few years, Archelaus had been removed from ruling Judea, which was instead ruled by Rome's appointed governors. Pilate was governor of Judea at the time of Jesus' crucifixion.

Mary told Luke the story of how Jesus had scared her and Joseph when he was only twelve years old. He got so wrapped up in the religious leaders' questions and answers that he stayed in the Temple courts while the rest of the Nazareth group headed home from the Passover Feast in Jerusalem. She smiled again thinking about their dismay in not finding him for three days, but he reminded them they should have known he would be in the Temple, his Father's house. Both Joseph and Mary were constantly aware of the fact that Mary was not Jesus' only parent! Events and thoughts she had stored in her heart for all these years came pouring out to Luke.

But now she was tired. She was, after all, seventy-four years old. She had a loving home with John here in Ephesus, where he was the lead elder of the growing church. Years before, Paul the Apostle had left early church leaders Priscilla and Aquila here to establish the church, and they had sent for John to continue the leadership of the church. Paul was now spending an extended time teaching here, although he was to leave soon. Luke, as Paul's newest traveling companion, would be leaving also.

John had cared for Mary from the moment Jesus had entrusted her to John as he hung upon the cross. Again the prophesy from Simeon, "a sword will pierce your very soul," went through her mind as she thought of the suffering she witnessed Jesus endure, yet he loved her so much he made sure she was cared for even as he was dying. And then Jesus was raised to life again! How amazing! How wonderful that God's plan of salvation was finally complete, and all who believe in Jesus' sacrifice and resurrection would have eternal life in heaven.

Mary sighed. What a full life she had lived! How gracious God had been to her! But she must rest now for Luke was coming the next day to talk with her again.

The following day, Luke again listened to Mary reminisce about her eventful life. She started again talking about her family — a typical family, it seemed, in the village of Nazareth. The boys learned the skills of building from their father, Joseph, and the girls learned skills of being a wife and caring for their future children. Mary's children were growing up, some married, when Joseph suddenly died. Mary didn't reveal how this happened, but she did say that Jesus became the head of the home and carefully tended to her and the children still at home. When they all had homes of their own — the sons had built their homes next to Joseph and Mary's home — Jesus went more often into the hills to commune with God the Father, to fast and pray. Then one time when he returned, Jesus told his mother he would be gone for a much longer time.

As she learned later, he went to where his cousin John was preaching and baptizing in the Jordan River. He was baptized by John, and as Jesus came up out of the water, the heavens opened, and John saw the Spirit of God descending like a dove and settling on Jesus. And a voice from heaven said, "This is my dearly loved Son, who brings me great joy."

This was the beginning of Jesus' ministry, when he was about thirty years old. Again, Luke carefully recorded more of Mary's remembrances of Jesus' life.

"His first miracle was turning water into wine at a family wedding in Cana," Mary said. "I was concerned that because of the larger-than-expected crowd, we had run out of wine. I knew Jesus' ministry was just starting — the first four of his disciples were with him. Perhaps a personal favor for his mother was not the proper way to announce his ministry to this group of people, but I was confident he would do the right thing, so I told the servants to do whatever he told them." She stopped and chuckled. "It was the best wine that had been served. My other sons and daughters and their families were there. They enjoyed the wine but couldn't quite believe that Jesus had made it from water! Thankfully, Jesus' disciples who were there put their faith in him because of this miracle.

"After the wedding, I went with Jesus, his disciples, and my other sons to Capernaum and spent a few wonderful days with my sister Salome and Zebedee, her husband, and their family. We all listened carefully to what Jesus was saying. I could see the Spirit truly was upon him.

"Jesus stopped by Nazareth occasionally during the first part of his ministry when he was in the area. The last time he visited in Nazareth, he again spoke at the synagogue on the Sabbath. At first my neighbors were amazed at his teaching, but they had watched him grow up and didn't accept his words as from God. Then when he said that no prophet is accepted in his own hometown, people got very upset, so upset that they forced him to the top of Mount Precipice planning to throw him over the cliff, but he passed right through the crowd. His brothers were there but they didn't defend him! After that, he made Capernaum his home base."

Mary told Luke that she stayed mainly in Nazareth during Jesus' ministry, but word often reached her and the village about his miracles and his teachings. "I rejoiced," Mary recalled, "but wished Joseph had lived to see the beginning of the fulfillment of the prophecies." Her son was the Son of God and was going to be, as the angel had said, on the "throne of his ancestor David, and he will reign over Israel forever; his Kingdom will never end."

"But," Mary admitted, "I still asked in my heart: How will Jesus' ministry, his miracles, result in a crown, a throne for him? When and how will he win over those who oppose him? Even though

"Every Knee Will Bow"

Jesus' teachings and miracles were touching hearts and gathering crowds, his heritage was questioned because he was raised in Nazareth. He didn't have proof he had been born in Bethlehem."

Mary's other sons also heard the reports about the Pharisees verbally attacking Jesus with great hostility in Jerusalem, in Judea, and in Galilee. The reports eventually said the Pharisees wanted to kill him because of his violation of the Pharisaic regulations about the Sabbath, and they were jealous that he drew large crowds. Though these reports concerned Mary, she was confident that somehow God would turn all these negatives into the final goal of a crown for him as the King of the Jews. Many who had tried to overthrow the Roman government had been defeated and killed, but Jesus was God's Son. His path to the "throne of his ancestor David" was certainly different than Mary and all others looking for the Messiah thought it would be.

One time Jesus' brothers took Mary with them when they went to talk with Jesus, perhaps to try to convince him that he needed to temper his ministry, or at least come home for a while. Mary said, "I guess they thought he might come speak to them because I was with them, but he was surrounded by people and didn't come out to speak with us. At that point, my heart was 'pierced by the sword' because my other sons didn't believe Jesus' teachings. They were expressing unbelief and even anger and shame at being related to him.

"Then when Jesus' ministry brought him nearby again, Jesus' brothers were able to speak to him," Mary recalled. "This was just before the Feast of Tabernacles. They said to Jesus, 'Leave here and go to Judea, where your followers can see your miracles! You can't become famous if you hide like this! If you can do such wonderful things, show yourself to the world.' They seemed almost to be taunting him to be 'famous' — they couldn't bring themselves to say 'King' or 'Messiah' — saying that he should reveal himself as such to the 'world,' probably meaning the religious leaders

Mary, the Lord's Servant

because obviously he was well known to his followers and the public. They still didn't believe in him. But Jesus told them, 'Now is not the right time for me to go.'

"But later he did go to the Feast of Tabernacles and taught in the Temple courts. Many people believed in him after listening to him, but his words also made the Pharisees and chief priests even more determined to arrest him and kill him. But it wasn't until months later when Jesus was in Jerusalem for the Passover that it all happened."

Mary paused, closed her eyes and sighed deeply. What she was about to recall for Luke was still, after all this time, so tender on her heart. Luke stopped her, knowing the telling of Jesus' crucifixion would be hard for Mary. He gently said to her, "I have interviewed several others, Mary. You don't have to tell me if you don't wish to."

"No, I want to tell you about the events as I saw them," Mary replied. Luke nodded.

"I traveled to Jerusalem with my son James and his family, along with my other sons, to go to Passover. I was confident that again Jesus and his disciples would be there, and he was. But I didn't see him until … until after he had been arrested. I was with James when someone came quickly to tell us Jesus had been arrested the night before, had already been sentenced to be crucified, and was being taken to the crucifixion site outside of the city. I jumped up to go at once. James tried to prevent me from leaving, but I knew I had to go. I had an idea where the disciples might be — they were gathered in a place called the Upper Room. Mary Magdalene was there, along with Salome, my sister, who is James' and John's mother. When I came in and said I wanted to go see Jesus, Mary Magdalene and Salome said they would go too, and John wanted to come along with us. We made our way to where the crowd was gathering and heard the soldiers driving the spikes into Jesus' hands and feet. John wouldn't let me watch, but after Jesus was hanging above us on the cross, I looked … and my heart broke in two. Indeed I felt like my heart was being pierced with a sword. So much pain and confusion at that point! It is hard to describe. People around us were jeering and yelling insults at Jesus. Other women who had traveled with the disciples came, too. We cried together.

"As he looked down, Jesus saw me there and saw John, too. He told John to take care of me. And he has from that very moment. When Jesus breathed his last, John led me and Salome and the other women away.

"What also pains my heart is that no one from my family, nor even his closest friends, asked for Jesus' body for burial. I suppose it would have been a dangerous thing for them to do. But a man named Joseph of Arimathea bravely asked permission from Pilate to bury Jesus' body. Looking back on that now, I do think that was God's will because he had a new tomb nearby. The next hours and days were heavy with sorrow and wondering how this was part of God's plan. I did not go back to James. I stayed with John and listened to the disciples in their sorrow and tears recount the times that Jesus recently had said that he would be killed. They told me that just one week previously, he had ridden into Jerusalem on a donkey, the sign of a king, and had been praised and greeted by an enormous, enthusiastic crowd. 'Blessings on the King who comes in the name of the Lord!' the crowd had cheered. But now he was dead, lying in a borrowed tomb."

Mary stopped talking, tears falling down her weathered cheeks as she remembered everyone's pain. Luke knew to allow Mary a moment of recalled grief. Then she straightened in her chair and took a deep breath.

"But ... BUT ..." She sighed and lifted her finger as if turning a page. Her countenance brightened. "This is where all our sorrow was turned to joy. Our tears of pain turned to tears of amazement and celebration.

"It was early in the morning on the first day of the week, three days later, when Mary Magdalene and a couple of other women

Mary, the Lord's Servant

took some burial spices to anoint Jesus' body since they knew he had been buried in haste. Of course they didn't know who was going to roll away that huge stone in front of the tomb. They left the place where we all were staying just as the sun was coming up. On their way there they felt an earthquake!

"Soon they came running back. I was there with the eleven disciples and some others. They told all of us that they had found the tomb open, and an angel told them Jesus had risen! 'He is alive!' the angel said. They had been so excited they didn't tell anyone until they got back to us. At first it didn't seem possible, but Peter and John left, running toward the tomb. They saw the grave clothes in the tomb, and they believed that Jesus was alive. Mary Magdalene again went to the tomb and lingered there. When she turned around, she saw Jesus. Alive! She saw him and talked with him!

"This was the first of several times he appeared, first to Mary Magdalene, then to two men who were walking to Emmaus, and that same evening he appeared to ten of the eleven remaining disciples. They of course were overjoyed and began to remember what Jesus had taught them about how he would suffer, die, but be raised to life again. Here's another amazing thing. Jesus appeared to James and to his other brothers. Suddenly they believed in him! Jesus appeared to his disciples in Galilee, on the shore of the Sea of Galilee, and to as many as five hundred of us believers at once. He taught us all to look at the prophecies about the Messiah in a new light.

"We had been looking for him as the Messiah to set up an earthly kingdom, like David's kingdom, but he reminded us that David had received the prophecy that his kingdom would last forever. A heavenly Kingdom. Jesus had said in his teachings that his kingdom is not of this world. Oh, he taught us all so many things and reminded the disciples what he had already taught them. He opened the minds of the disciples and all the believers so we could understand the Scriptures.

"Every Knee Will Bow"

"After forty days, he told us to 'stay in Jerusalem until we had been clothed with power from on high.' Then he led his disciples and other believers to the Mount of Olives toward Bethany, lifted up his hands and blessed us. While he was blessing us, he was taken up into heaven. After he was gone and we stood wondering at what we had seen, two angels appeared next to us and said, 'Why are you standing here staring into heaven? Jesus has been taken from you into heaven, but someday he will return from heaven in the same way you saw him go!' Oh, how we praised Jesus! We returned to Jerusalem with great joy. We went day after day to the temple to praise God.

"Just ten days after Jesus ascended into heaven, on the day of the Pentecost festival, while the disciples and other believers, including Jesus' brothers and me, were at the temple praising God, His Holy Spirit was poured out on all of us — one hundred and twenty of us gathered at that time. His coming sounded like a mighty wind and tongues like fire rested on each of us. It was an amazing time of accepting the power of the infilling of the Holy Spirit.

"People from all over the world were in Jerusalem for the Feast of Pentecost. They heard the sound of the wind but didn't feel any wind. They were bewildered when they heard all of us praising God in different languages, even their own, languages we had not learned. They were utterly amazed. Peter addressed the crowd and told them about this being a fulfillment of prophecy and told them about Jesus. He invited them to accept Jesus as Savior, and three thousand — three thousand of them! — repented and became followers that day! It was the beginning of many more people believing in Jesus as Lord and Savior.

"The power of the Holy Spirit continues to bring many to believe in Jesus. What we then understood from the Scriptures was that Jesus came, the Son of God, the Savior, so that all who believe in him, all who believe he has risen from the dead, can have forgiveness of sins. We need only to ask for forgiveness. This is

Mary, the Lord's Servant

the Kingdom; we can all be part of the Kingdom, Jew and Gentile alike. One day, like the angels who appeared after Jesus' ascension into heaven said, Jesus will return. At that time every knee will bow before him! Every knee! How much better to bow now in worship than to bow then in judgment!

"There have been times of persecution. Only a short time after Jesus ascended into heaven, James, the disciple (my nephew), was martyred, and soon many believers were forced to leave Jerusalem. But God has used that as well because wherever believers have gone, they have told others about Jesus, and knowledge about him and belief in his sacrifice have spread far and wide, and it continues. You know about that, Luke, as a traveling companion of Paul. This church in Ephesus is growing because of Paul's teaching.

"My son James became the head of the church in Jerusalem but may soon have to leave because of another wave of persecution. Luke, please continue to tell the story of Jesus. Many more people than just Theophilus will read your account of the good news and they, too, will believe in Jesus' deep love and great sacrifice just for them."

Mary closed her eyes, smiled, and sighed. "Soon my life on earth will end, but I am looking forward to being in heaven with Jesus. I will rejoice forever in his Kingdom with all those who believe in him. I know I will receive a warm welcome and an embrace from my son, but first I want to kneel and worship him as my Lord and Savior."

APPENDIX

Scriptures used:

    Genesis 18; 30
    Leviticus 12
    Numbers 6:24-26
    1 Samuel 1
    Psalm 59:16-17; 91:1, 11-12
    Isaiah 9:6-7; 7:14
    Micah 5:2
    Matthew 1:16 – 2:23; 3:13-17; 27:57-61
    Luke 1:1--2:52; 3:23-24; 4:14-30; 19:29-38; 23:35; 24
    Mark 3:31-33; 6:3; 15:40-41; 16:1-20
    John 7:1-14, 31-32, 19:25-27; 20; 21
    Acts 1:1-11; 2:1-41; 5:37; 18:1-21; 19